Business Straight to the Heart

The Remodelers Guide to Leadership,
Management and Success

By Linda Case

Business Straight to the Heart

The Remodelers Guide to Leadership, Management and Success

By Linda Case

Published by

14440 Cherry Lane Court, Suite 201
Laurel, Maryland 20707

First printing 2011
Printed in the United States of America
ISBN: 978-0-9838151-0-5

Cover and book design by A Scribbler's Press, Ltd.
ascribblerspress.com

Remodelers Advantage, Inc.
14440 Cherry Lane Court Suite 201
Laurel, Maryland 20707
www.remodelersadvantage.com

table
of contents

introduction: How lucky you are iii

chapter 1: Where *is* the Owner's Manual? 1

chapter 2: Learning and Earning Leadership 39

chapter 3: Building A Great Team 61

chapter 4: Managing to the Max 105

chapter 5: Planning to Succeed 133

chapter 6: Magnetic Marketing 157

chapter 7: When Business Gives You Lemons 175

introduction

HOW LUCKY YOU ARE to be reading this book! In 1971, when I first turned to carpentry to put bread on my table, there was really only one way to learn the craft: team up with an experienced craftsman, watch him carefully, and try to duplicate exactly what you saw. Questions were asked sparingly, and the answers often only added to the confusion. I was luckier than most because I first worked with a crew of design-build students who were thoughtful about what they were doing and why they were doing it. It was a time of innovation, particularly in the area of energy efficiency and especially in the harsh climate of Vermont. But learning was still mainly a matter of imitation, an informal apprenticeship system that perpetuated sound principles of construction practice when the "teacher" got it right and unsound principles when he got it wrong.

Like many who enter the remodeling business, the better I became technically, the more questions I got from homeowners about problems they had with their homes or changes they wanted to make. I quickly discovered that craft was just the tip of the remodeling iceberg. As projects grew in size, I needed to establish credit with suppliers, develop relationships with trade contractors, hire and manage employees, develop estimates, sell the jobs, write contracts, send invoices, keep the books, and look for more work.

Unfortunately, there was even less of an education system for the business side of remodeling than there was for the craft side. Contractors would meet at the counter at the suppliers and exchange pleasantries, but no one ever revealed how much work they had in the pipeline or how much they were paying their crew or how much profit they were making.

The fact is, most weren't really keeping track and didn't know the answers to critical business questions. They judged a new job according to how similar it was to a past job and then charged a little more for it this year than they did last year and hoped for the best. They never paid themselves directly, so they didn't really know how much they were earning for all the hours they were spending. And they never kept track of job costs, so they didn't find out whether or not they'd broken even until tax time.

All of that changed in the early 1980's with the publication of two magazines devoted to the craft and business of building and remodeling. One was *New England Builder*, better known today as *The Journal of Light Construction*. JLC was full of first-person accounts of real-world jobsite problems and practical, field-tested know-how. It was the first forum in which contractors could talk with each other about common problems without having to worry about being competitive.

The other publication was *Remodeling* magazine, which did for the business side what JLC did for the technical side. The magazine's mission was clearly articulated through two regular columnists. One was Walt Stoeppelwerth, whose big-picture perspective gave vision to an industry that was struggling to find its identity. Walt was an innovator, a champion of the entrepreneur, who taught a generation of remodelers how to place value on the service they performed.

The other columnist was Linda Case. Linda's early columns appeared under the heading "Image," and while the advice she dispensed about marketing and public relations was on point, it quickly became clear that her expertise extended into every nook and cranny of a remodeling company's business. She knew her readers were literally doing everything in their company that needed to be done, and she knew they needed help. So she determined to help them with everything.

And help them she did. Not just with her expertise, but with their own hard-won experiences. She showed remodelers that there was an advantage to sharing what they had learned, both the successes and the failures. She helped them see that it was impossible to know too much, and that educating yourself and your team was an essential part of being in business.

The result was Remodelers Advantage, one of the first peer-to-peer networking groups in the nation, an organization that formalized Linda's vision of remodelers helping remodelers by sharing their knowledge, their fears, and their successes.

And that's why you're so lucky to be reading this book. It brings together the insights, analysis, and accumulated wisdom from Linda Case's decades-long interaction with hundreds of working remodeling contractors who have, under her tutelage, transformed their "accidental businesses" into successful, directed companies leading the way into a new era of enterprise.

I've had the great privilege of working with Linda since I joined *Remodeling* magazine 10 years ago, and I can tell you that there isn't a speck of presumption or ego in anything she writes, says, or does. Read her book carefully and often; like the author, it's the genuine article.

Sal Alfano
Editorial Director, *Remodeling* magazine

chapter one

WHERE *IS* THE OWNER'S MANUAL?

The Right Questions

And More Questions

Never-Ending Transitions

Evolution or Revolution?

Business Potholes

More Business Potholes

Developing a Framework
for Success

Creating Peace of Mind

The Very Best Practices

Right Question = Right Solution

Put a Little Zingerman's
in Your Business

Influencing

Multitasking to the Max

Pillow Talk

Passing On

Help is Only a Consultant Away

"Watch, listen, and learn. You can't know it all yourself. Anyone who thinks they do is destined for mediocrity."

Donald Trump

YOU BUY A COFFEEMAKER, OR A VACUUM, or nearly anything and what accompanies it? An owner's manual with easy start-up instructions and a troubleshooting chart. You buy or start a company and there you are in an empty room with an empty file cabinet and a computer and some supplies. There is no owner's manual and certainly no troubleshooting chart.

One of your biggest quests as a business owner is to answer some very basic questions:

➤ What are your personal strengths and weaknesses?

➤ What kind of a company are you best suited to run?

➤ How will that company be unique in the marketplace?

➤ Will that uniqueness sell? Is there a market for it?

Let's start with the first question. What are your personal strengths and weaknesses? For most of my early years as a consultant, I worked to bolster the weaknesses of my clients. I slowly learned that they could only modify their natural style. They couldn't morph from gazelles into leopards. So I turned my efforts to encouraging them to lead with their strengths while bolstering their weaker sides.

Often, that bolstering can be provided by hiring those who will for instance, organize the unorganized owners. Or hiring a draftsperson for those who can sell but don't enjoy the final detailed designing.

So don't beat yourself up on this one. The best we can hope for is to do a number of roles well, recognize that we need help in other areas, and find that support.

As to answering "What kind of a company am I best suited to run," the answer is partly found in the answer to the first question but also to "What do you enjoy doing?" What are you passionate about? If you love building beautiful contemporary renovations, or you are passionate about energy efficiency, or you just love helping people achieve their dreams, the kernel of the answer probably lies with those feelings. Take some time to daydream. Create a vision that is so strong, so tangible that you can feel it, smell it, taste it, and act to realize it.

If you are just starting out, you'll still probably have to respond to all requests, whether they fit your dream or not, but hold tight to that vision and move toward it bit by bit. The strongest remodelers are those who know who they are and what they are best at.

But, and it's a big but, your market has to have enough buyers who respond to your unique offering. The market is always right. So the fourth question you must answer is "will your uniqueness sell?"

The big "aha" here is to dare to create the company that plays to your strengths and your passions. If you do this well, your buyer will love your enthusiasm and the unique personality of your company. You won't have any real competitors and your work will be a labor of love.

The Right Questions

Are you wondering what you will do "when you grow up"? Are you feeling blah about your business and where you are in life? Do you wonder if there is more (satisfaction? money? free time? balance? fun?) than you are currently experiencing?

No, this is not a commercial for hair implants, little blue pills, or a singles dating service. It is not uncommon for me to work with remodelers who question the direction they have taken in their business lives. So what do I do? I ask them *more* questions.

This may sound like a fortune cookie, but I've learned over the years that the right answers come from asking the right questions. And the right answers come from reaching back to the bedrock in your life (what you love, what you believe, what is really important to you) and then working forward.

Here are some tried-and-true questions that I use to help elicit answers from clients that can point the way to the company that best suits their abilities and lifestyle. You can use them, too. Just be sure to write down your answers so you can adjust and edit them and return to them in order to mine the information they hold for you. To give you some idea of how your answer might look, I've provided a few of the answers recently given by a remodeler in his quest for a better fit with his company.

What are your strengths and weaknesses as a person?

What are your strengths and weaknesses in business?
"I tend to take on too much. I over-commit. I fail to follow through....I am sometimes almost visionary. I am particularly creative, resourceful, and a great problem solver. And I have always been exceptional at bringing in business...but not so good at handling it once I've brought it in."

What do you love to do in your personal life?

What do you love to do at work?

What do you dislike doing at work?

"I hate being disorganized or not on top of my details. I also dislike being hectic, particularly because I tend to lose focus when I am hectic and then I can miss important things. I get tired and bored when doing repetitive tasks...."

If you had just the company you want 3 years from now, what would it look like?

How do you like managing others in your business? Are you good at hiring? At coaching?
"I like managing. I can be a good coach, and I can tell people hard things, too, when necessary, usually in a productive way. I do, however, need a good structure to make sure I follow through on all of the details...."

What kind and size of projects please you the most?

What kind of clients (including education level, finances) do you prefer working with?

Do you read business books? How many in a year? If so which have been your favorites?

Do you read trade magazines, trade books, etc.?

How do you view the importance of finances in your company? How do you judge if you are doing well or poorly financially?
"It's as if I have had blinders on these last 6 years. All I paid attention to was the checkbook balance, my billables, and what I was able to draw out as take-home pay....I understand that to move forward I must discipline myself to pay close and regular attention to the P&L and the balance sheet...."

Each of us can design a company that complements our goals and talents. It takes stepping back, analyzing what is working and what is not, assessing our strengths and weaknesses, and then building a company where our strengths are maximized to their highest impact and value—and one where we love what we do and what we deliver!

And More Questions....

The following is the quickest quiz you'll ever take. It will take you approximately 10 seconds. If you can answer "yes" to the following three questions, you don't need to read any further. Pat yourself on the back, for you are a success in business. However, if some of your answers are "no," keep reading.

1. Do you make a good salary and a net profit that compensates you for the risks you take as owner?

2. Do you work 50 hours a week or less in your business?

3. Are you generally happy in your business?

The last question is undoubtedly the most important but is usually dependent on the first two. So let's start with money.

1. Can a remodeler make both a good salary *and* a healthy net profit of 5 to 10%? Absolutely. Is it easy? Not particularly. But it's not easy to be financially successful in any field. After working with thousands of remodelers, I have learned that turning this critical area around starts with convincing the owner that there is no use staying in their business if they can't make adequate money (the "stick") and showing them that others no brighter or more talented than they have conquered this problem (the "carrot").

Here is my prescription:
➤ Read *The E Myth Revisited* by Michael Gerber.
➤ Read *The Remodelers Guide to Making and Managing Money.*
➤ Be sure you get monthly profit & loss statements and a balance sheet and have them explained to you as many times as necessary so that you fully understand them and could explain them to someone else.
➤ Join a local association, go to every meeting, and absorb every bit of learning available.
➤ Start a monthly breakfast (or lunch, or dinner) club with non-competing remodelers and share information.
➤ Find a mentor in the community who is willing to help you. They may be another business owner, a father, a sister, or whatever. Meet monthly.

➤ Go to The Remodeling Show, held annually each fall, and attend every financially oriented workshop. Aim to meet other remodelers from around the country with whom you can stay in touch.

➤ Join our Remodelers Advantage Roundtables peer group, where non-competing remodelers from around the country meet to share the successes and the challenges of their businesses.

2. Can a remodeler keep to a 50-hour-a-week schedule—or less? Absolutely. And, listen carefully: I have never seen a company falter whose owner cut their hours back to a reasonable level. You may have to hire help or stop doing some tasks or delegate better. But there is a way around your overwork. Plus, when you work reasonable hours, you will work smarter and better. Here are some ideas:

➤ Assess just how you are spending your time at work. You may even have to keep a 2-week log. Knowing where your time is going will quickly lead you to some solutions.

➤ Consider what you could (and should) delegate to others in your company. Do you have a production manager and yet you still have significant involvement in production? Do you have the wrong person and that's why you aren't delegating? Or are you a control freak who has trouble letting go? Take the appropriate action.

➤ Consider what you could (and should) subcontract out. Are you spending lots of time designing and drafting? Could that be transferred to someone who would work on an "as needed" basis? Marketing is often easily subcontracted. If you, the owner, are doing the bookkeeping, consider outsourcing those duties. Your time is worth at least $50 an hour. If you are doing the work of a $15-an-hour person, stop.

➤ Are there time-absorbers that could be avoided with better prevention? For instance, sometimes production occupies an owner's time because he/she hasn't put a comprehensive sales package together that delivers the right information in a timely manner to the field.

➤ Are you working 10-hour days and selling at night? This has two effects — you are tired when you are selling and your hours go on overload. You have two choices: Stop selling at night or take compensatory time off during the day for the night hours. I recommend the first option.

3. Is it possible for a remodeler to really enjoy their work? Of course it is. Adequate compensation and reasonable hours are a great start. But sometimes they aren't enough. Here are some ideas:

➤ Assess just what parts of the work you do that you really enjoy. Is there a way to let you do more of that and less of what you don't enjoy? If you like to sell but hate to estimate, how can you delegate estimating? And to whom?

➤ Consider taking a special vacation meant to recharge your batteries. Leave your phone number with the office but do not call them. Let them call you if there is an emergency.

➤ Get away from your company and think how you can redesign your company to make you happier.

➤ Hire a general manager who will run the company day-to-day and will let you govern from the board of directors level. With good middle management you'd be able to pursue other opportunities (this sounds much easier than it really is, but it is quite possible). Your company volume probably has to be $2 million or above to do this.

These are three of the biggest challenges in remodeling. But they are very conquerable. Don't despair; just attack.

Never-Ending Transitions

Billy Keenan was in a bind. His gut was telling him that how he was spending his time as owner of W.J. Keenan Building Contractor in Piscataway, N.J., was going to kill his beloved company. "For 30 years all my pleasure has come from my work on the jobsite," he says. "But the more work I did, the more trouble I got into. I was having so much fun framing jobs that I'd forget to call the plumber. I would leave sales and estimating for the late night hours or weekends."

Keenan is not alone. He, and his business, are undergoing a normal transition. Studies show that companies go through two-part phases as they grow. They settle into a mode that works for their current volume and operation and that creates peace and prosperity for a while. Then, as their size increases, they outgrow that phase and chaos ensues. Their systems that worked before no longer are a good fit for what they are doing now. Their personnel may not have the ability or inclination to learn new higher level skills. Their trusty, loyal office manager now becomes a problem employee. The technically great carpenter can't master running a job, using the computer system, and filling out and turning in the paperwork.

If you've been through one of these transition points, you've suddenly gone from running smoothly to running rough. The business, and your skills as owner, have to be reinvented to meet the new challenges. The key is to know that this is normal in business. You, as owner, will forever be on the learning curve. Let's see what Bill Keenan, who also has a way with words, has to say about his new challenges.

"I started this company by trading a crushed fender on my car for a power saw," says Bill. "A Skil worm drive, to be exact. I saw more potential in that old saw than I did in a new fender. That being said, I have now come to a crossroads in my journey. I now must leave what I know and do so well to point my company in the proper direction to help it grow and prosper. The old process has only taken me so far. This step is taken with much trepidation. Fear of the unknown causes a falter in my step. It will take much perseverance on my part and much patience and prodding on the part of others. I will mourn the passing of those calloused hands. But not unlike that old saw, I see potential here."

Keenan's transition includes four major changes:

➤ His wife, Tina, came in "mega fulltime" to organize the office, schedule jobs, design kitchens and baths, and generally create a more systematized organization.

➤ Keenan raised the priority of his role as salesperson and estimator and now does that work during the week rather than fitting it into odd hours.

➤ The couple joined our Remodelers Advantage Roundtables program, where they meet semi-annually with similar company owners to share challenges and commitments. "I wanted to meet guys like me who had jumped this taking-off-the-toolbelt hurdle," explains Keenan.

➤ Hardest of all, Keenan now divides his time equally between the office and the field.

Bill and Tina's company is relatively small but the lesson to be learned from them is universal. Your company is an ever-changing organism, so you as owner have to be one, too. Keep alert for when what has worked for you in the past stops working. The needs of your company for leadership and direction now call for you to learn new skills. You'll be on the learning curve...forever. And that's a good thing.

Evolution or Revolution?

Once upon a time, many years ago, an industry insider told me that no remodeling company would ever grow over a million in volume. So much for making predictions. Many remodelers grapple with the growth issue and often ask me about this option.

Tell me you want to grow your company and my next questions are always the same. Why? How? When? Not because I don't think it's a great idea, but because there are good reasons to grow and poor reasons to grow. I'm not talking about the 5% or 10% annual growth that is evolutionary. Rather, I'm focusing on that 25%-plus annual growth rate, which is revolutionary.

Good "why" answers for me include answers like, "Growth would support my personal goals," or "I want to leave a legacy," or "I want to have a company that can be sold," or "I want to build critical mass that allows for career advancement for my staff." Answers that concern me are "because it's there," or "I need to grow my way to profitability," or "I simply want to be the biggest in my market."

Many folks want to know the best way to grow quickly. There actually are a number of routes. You could raise your average job size, which for many companies can be the simplest and least disturbing. You could add a new profit center, increase your geographical area, or just do more of the type of work you already do. Or you could join forces with another company, which can work but may be the most problematic way to grow. You are adding the complexity of working with a new partner to the complexity of growth.

The "when" of growth—your timing—is also key. Here are some *caution signals* that would say slow down and get your house in order before you grow substantially:

➤ Your company does not consistently reach an annual net profit of 5% or more.

➤ Your company has poor infrastructure. Your employees are not harnessed to work toward company goals. Accountability is weak. Systems are spotty.

➤ You do not have a strategic plan and vision for the business.

➤ You are not managing by the numbers using accurate P&L's, balance sheets, job-cost reports, and budgets.

➤ You are not using a professional level markup—most likely in the 50% to 67% range. This markup is what you will need to buy the increased overhead and allow for a net profit each year.

Many business experts feel that if you grow without getting rid of the above problems, that your "baggage" will substantially increase your risk of failure.

But let's be more positive. What are some of the signals that might give you a green light to increasing volume substantially?

➤ The market is signaling that it will support your growth. You have strong leads and a good backlog of work in the 3-to-6-month range. The economic outlook in your community is bright.

➤ Your company is thriving at its current level.

➤ A larger company will fit your vision both personally and professionally.

➤ You have staff ready to grow, willing to grow, and craving the career advancement that comes from growth.

➤ As owner, you can and will delegate. You will be able to see your primary role as coaching the team. You have a key management team in place that meets regularly to work on the business.

Growth is a journey, not a destination. As Eric Flamholtz and Yvonne Randle describe the journey in their book, *Growing Pains*, "The sea is unfamiliar, the boat is clumsy, the skills needed are not readily apparent or not fully developed, and there is a constant reminder of the high costs of an error in judgment."

But growth is an exciting adventure into new territory. Just be sure you are as prepared as you possibly can be. Happy sailing, and don't forget the life jackets.

Business Potholes

As a remodeler, you've undoubtedly worked with many clients and prospects who come to you with misunderstandings or "myths" they have about remodeling and remodelers. I thought I'd focus this essay on some of the myths I hear over and over from remodelers about their businesses that I don't think are true.

The first myth is one that many of the motivational books will try to teach you: If you do good work, the money will come. Or if you do what you love, the money will come. Or even that if you think the right thoughts, the money will come. Certainly doing good work and crafting your designs and projects well are a given if you want to succeed. But you and I know that the client would rather pay $35,000 than $50,000 for that well-crafted project, or $25,000 or $10,000. We can't expect the client to be educated on the true value of our work. We have to be in charge of what we get paid.

And I am such a firm believer in loving what you do. However, that can be a real trap because it leads to fear that if you charge what you should charge, you won't get to do what you love. Have you ever fallen in love with a project and then been tempted to lower the price so you will get it? Or maybe you rationalize that you may not make much money on it, but it will be a great marketing tool. After all, it's in the right neighborhood and the photos may lead to awards and more.

You are in business to make money while doing good work and loving at least 75% of what you do. So don't put the cart before the horse—or expect that if you have a cart, a horse will appear.

I first heard this next myth in 1982, when I started working with remodelers. Bless Walt Stoeppelwerth, who believed in me and let me join him on the seminar circuit. He had been a voice crying in the desert, subject to scorn, argued with constantly, who worked tirelessly to sell the concept of a professional level markup (a 50% to 67% markup leading to a 33% to 40% gross profit). Maybe you've even been a disbeliever in the past but if you're still in business, you converted.

Over and over we heard, "You can't charge those crazy markups," or "Maybe in someone else's market that will work but not in mine!" And still today, as each wave of new remodelers rolls in, the same phrase persists.

What's the solution? Simply do an annual budget. Look at the real costs of running your business, add in a reasonable salary for yourself and net profit, and see what it costs you. Then mark up based on that information. What we know is that you'll be pretty close to that same professional level markup we taught in the 1980's.

This third widespread myth is about those folks you know and love—your staff. Most of us, since we haven't had a lot of experience working in a variety of companies, hold a very erroneous and harmful (to ourselves) notion. We believe our employees are raw clay, which we can knead and massage into just what we want them to be—sort of like stem cells that can grow into a variety of types of cells. So Joe the estimator is a pretty good guy. We all like him. Let's turn him into our production manager.

Do we have a production manager job description? No. Have we spent some time considering what that position requires in talent, temperament, and people skills? No. Have we scoured our market for a star? No. And Mary's been a great all-around receptionist/clerk and we need a bookkeeper. There we go again.

Well folks, people are not clay, staffing is not a plug-and-play activity, and people arrive at your door with their unique talents, skills, and baggage. A great bookkeeper is a smart, highly detail-oriented single tasker and is able to spend an hour chasing down that missing penny.

Jim Collins, the great business author (*Good to Great, Built to Last*), talks of having the right people in the right seats on your bus. And that bus is your business. So when you have an opening in your company, don't be a potter working with clay trying to invent the candidate from what you have on board. Be a sports team scout making it youir business to find the very best talent that the team can afford to pay in that key position. Your ability to deliver well, delight clients, and make money depends on it.

So know that there are many parts to making money in this business and there are no shortcuts. Know that you first must understand and believe in the value you bring to your client. Build that incredible team from the best players in your market. Then go get that sleek, shiny bus to drive for success.

More Business Potholes

Here are six more myths that could act as stumbling blocks to your company's success. Let's start out with a few more staffing presumptions that I run into.

Hiring family members will be the right choice because I can trust them, they're available, and they need the work.

There are so many examples of this hypothesis gone wrong, and a few where it has proven itself. If you formalize the job structure with a job description and metrics for success, advertise it externally and internally ,and find your relative is the absolute best choice, you are a lucky business owner. Be sure to have an agreement with them that your relationship in business is a different one from your personal relationship. In plain language, that means you will be able to fire them if there is not a good fit but you'll still be able to maintain your personal relationship with them.

My spouse will be a great bookkeeper/office manager/production manager (fill in the blank)—and she/he will be so happy working with me.

Many spouses have saved many remodeling companies. But many spouses, when you dig a little deeper, really yearn for a career of their own. Be sure to do that digging and really listen to the answers. If other fields look greener to your spouse, work out a transition that keeps your business safe but lets them see the light at the end of the tunnel.

Yes, I'm the only one who gets paid, but my spouse understands that it's really compensation for both of us.

Often, accountants recommend apportioning the pay in a way that is beneficial for reducing taxes. If they recommend that one person be highly paid and the other paid minimally, I often see an underlying dissatisfaction in the latter spouse. But what happens to the motivation for money in your spouse? What happens to the earnings record for your spouse? Check with your accountant about whether you both could switch off who is higher paid and who is lower paid from year to year.

I'm not good at reading financials, but my bookkeeper understands them.

Whoops! I'd hate to count the number of bookkeeper embezzlements that I have heard about, much less those that have happened in the entire industry. In addition, the vast majority of company bookkeepers (not all) are very savvy about getting those numbers accurate but not savvy about interpreting the meaning of those numbers on your business' present and future. It's key to business success that you understand the meaning of each and every major entry on your P&L and balance sheet. You must be the financial manager for your company.

And speaking of money...

I'm careful to plan out and estimate each job accurately, so I really don't have a need to do a budget for my company.
The truth is, every job can go beautifully and according to plan, and you can have a losing year if you don't have enough volume or if the gross profit you planned and achieved was not enough to cover your overhead and provide you with an 8 to 10% net. You need estimating and monitoring of actual results in two areas—at the job level and at the company level.

Whenever I discern a difficult client during the sales process, I put an extra 10% on the job.
What you can earn on a job is a limited number, but what you can lose is unlimited. A cranky client costs you money, time, and morale. I regularly hear of jobs where only the owner can go back to do the work because the carpenters and trade contractors are worn out or not allowed on the job.

The sales process is the "dating" phase of remodeling. We all are or should be on our best behavior. A prospect who is outside the pleasantness norm at that stage is likely to be very unpleasant during the heat of construction. Commit to politely saying "thanks, but no thanks" as soon as you've made the diagnosis.

You've been warned. Potholes ahead.

Developing a Framework for Success

What is success and what are the key steps to achieving success? Let's start by defining success in a general way—you can add your personal take to the list (sailing around the world, sending all four of your kids to college debt free, saving so you can retire at 60...). I think we can agree that these four are important ingredients:

➤ A healthy net profit year-after-year

➤ Above-average compensation for the owner

➤ Working hours that allow for a balanced life

➤ Building a significant company that contributes value to clients, employees, other business partners, and the community

I suspect you won't argue over any of those four. Now what practices/processes are key to your achieving that success? Here are my candidates:

➤ Creating leadership at all levels

➤ Gathering accurate, timely information

➤ Setting S.M.A.R.T. goals

➤ Executing effectively through people and systems

➤ Measuring and assessing your progress constantly

It all begins with *Leadership.* Company owners must lead or else someone else in the company will, but obviously they won't choose to go where the owner wants. In the best of companies, that leadership is shared so that every employee is empowered to lead those they work with and supervise. Some of this leadership may well be vested in a key management team which helps to govern.

But always, leadership comes from the top and includes such things as defining and teaching the vision, mission, and core values of the company and modeling the behaviors desired in the company. It's holding steady at the tiller when the company is in rough seas. It's coaching, mentoring, cheerleading, and making tough calls when they have to be made.

After leadership, *gathering accurate and timely information* is an important starting point. We can't correct what we don't know about. We have to have accurate and timely information about many aspects of the company—

financial, sales, marketing, estimating, and lots more. I find that this foundation is usually missing or faulty when remodelers first come to me for help. Once we get regular financials, marketing and lead statistics, and productivity figures, we are ready to get into a cycle of continuous improvement. No matter the condition of your company when you start on this important loop, good information enables you to get better and better and eventually arrive at success.

Having that leadership and information propels us into the continuous improvement loop. With the information gathered, we can move to *setting S.M.A.R.T. (specific, measurable, attainable, realistic, and time-based) goals.* Those goals are often carried within a business plan, a budget, a marketing plan, marketing budget and calendar, departmental improvements, increased client satisfaction, and more. By using the S.M.A.R.T. system, all goals include practical definitions of success so that we'll clearly know when we achieve them. This simple discipline banishes the New Year's resolution style goal setting, which is so fleeting and ineffective.

Now that we know where we want to go, *effective execution* is the key. But for many of us, it is by far the hardest. We make paper plans but don't turn them into reality. There are two important sets of contributors to successful execution—a top-performing and empowered team that has bought into those goals and systems, and procedures that create consistent results. Having empowered performers on our team who are utilizing well-designed systems is a major accomplishment in any business, but one that pays off handsomely in delivering well, and in freeing up the owner.

The third step in the continuous improvement cycle is *measuring and assessing constantly.* These tell us how we are doing on executing our goals. Because we accompanied our goals with metrics, we can now get reports that will allow us to monitor our progress or lack thereof. For instance, did we want to improve our close ratio from 1 sale per 8 qualified leads to 1 per 7? We'll have made sure that close ratio is measured and we can assess our progress.

We've done the full loop, but that means it's time to go around again. Take that close ratio example. Maybe we are only halfway to the goal—now we are closing 1 sale out of every 7.5 leads. We reset the goal in a S.M.A.R.T. format, execute, remeasure, and keep improving. And the improvement cycles, like the wheels on the bus, go round and round.

Creating Peace of Mind

Want to be Santa Claus any time during the year? Want to give your family and your business some very special gifts? Or do you just want to be a responsible business owner and spouse? How does increasing their security and peace of mind sound? The dictionary definitions for security include freedom from anxiety and fear and a defense against financial failure—not very glamorous maybe, but a very big gift.

Here are five personal protections:

➤ I have an up-to-date will/estate plan in effect that includes how my business would be handled if I die. Both I and my spouse understand the provisions and agree to it.

➤ My spouse and I have an insurance package appropriate for our stage in life and the age of any children. We also have an umbrella insurance policy to extend any liability coverage we might need and to protect our assets.

➤ And have gotten expert, fee-only financial help in planning what we have to save every year in order to achieve our goals. We are on track.

➤ My spouse and I treat our personal bookkeeping like a business. We track it via simple software, know what it costs us to live and play each year, and are able to budget each year in advance.

➤ I have a list of all suppliers where I have signed personally for the account. I am working hard to meet any qualifications that will concentrate all business debt in the business.

Here are five business protections:

➤ I know how much "running money" the company needs to operate successfully and I keep the company cash down to that level. I have a credit line for when there are seasonal adjustments. I review this monthly or quarterly.

➤ I have had all relevant company forms and documents reviewed by an attorney with the appropriate specialty (construction, employment, tax) and made any requested changes.

➤ I have taken simple steps to protect the company against embezzlement. These include never signing blank checks, never authorizing the use of a "signature" stamp, staying conversant with who our subs and suppliers are, and signing checks only when they are attached to the supporting invoices.

➤ Also, to protect the company against embezzlement, I am still the person who opens and reviews the bank statements directly and I have made sure that our accounting software has been adapted (if necessary) so that it cannot be modified by staff without a record.

➤ I have protected my clients, my employees, my company, and my family by having every new prospective employee undergo a pre-employment screening by an outside firm, which includes drug testing, a driving record check, and a criminal record check.

If there are any of these you couldn't check off, go for it!

We have two experts to thank for help with this information: Glenn Henderson, CPA, of Henderson Edwards Wilson and Walt Mathieson, CPA, of Mathieson Consulting, Inc.

The Very Best Practices

Research in our industry is scarce and so should be taken seriously. Recently, we surveyed the business practices of 172 remodelers in our Roundtables program. These are remodelers who are biased toward improvement through education and who are actively seeking changes that will make their businesses even more successful. They are not a random group. However, they do vary in how well they apply the tools they learn in our program. Walt Mathieson, CPA, of Mathieson Consulting compiled the results. Here is what we discovered:

Successful firms (those that ranked in the top 10% of our measures of success) differed from firms that are struggling to succeed (those ranking in the bottom 10%) in the following ways:

➤ They are more likely to use percentage of completion accounting.

➤ They do less work priced on a time and materials basis.

➤ They review their job cost reports more frequently.

➤ They perform job "autopsies" consistently, carefully analyzing the financial outcomes of projects.

➤ Their average job size is significantly larger.

➤ They use a larger markup percentage in their estimating and pricing model, even at the expense of poorer closing ratios.

➤ They have less job-cost slippage between what they estimate and what they achieve.

➤ While they may fail to meet their projected gross sales goals, they miss their sales goal by a smaller percentage.

➤ Their overhead often was lower than projected in their budgets (or they missed it by less).

➤ They consistently come close to meeting or they exceed their company budget goals.

➤ They have a larger backlog of work, providing them security and allowing them to sell with less pressure.

➤ They have nearly twice the revenue per employee. This may reflect increased efficiency but is also because more of their job costs are subcontracted.

➤ They spend more on marketing, both in gross dollars and as a percentage of sales.

➤ More of their work is negotiated rather than competitively bid.

➤ They also more fully use our Remodelers Advantage Roundtables Tools (nine internal processes, such as faithful attendance at meetings, ability to make and achieve stretch commitments, etc.) and they master Roundtables Success Practices (reviewing and understanding their financials, having accurate financials in the percentage of completion format, producing a realistic annual budget for the company that is updated quarterly, and combining accurate estimating with timely job-cost reports carefully reviewed.)

Because of their success, the top 10% in our study reaped the following rewards:

➤ More total compensation

➤ Significantly higher working capital

➤ Significantly higher current ratio (more current assets than current liabilities)

➤ Significantly higher net worth

➤ Generally higher owner satisfaction levels

Top remodelers plan for their success in the careful preparation of meaningful and realistic budgets, and then execute their plan, monitoring progress against that plan. They also take care to control job costs and overhead costs, minimizing slippage in both. They are willing to ask for higher markups when pricing their work. They spend more for marketing and tend to plan and execute their marketing effectively. Making money—and having greater satisfaction—in remodeling is all about good business practices. And that means considerable time and effort and money spent in developing those practices and making them habitual in the company. The benefits are outstanding.

Right Question = Right Solution

I've often said (and believed) that asking the right question will lead you to the right answer. Recently, Kraig Kramers, a dynamic speaker and author of the book *CEO Tools*, gave a presentation for our clients. He sparked heated discussions and many comments through the use of two questions. I think these questions, in light of the current recession, have become critical to the survival of our businesses. Spending some serious thought and time on them might help your business, too.

The first question is, "What causes sales in your organization?" Kramers wasn't looking only for the tried-and-true answers like, "Well, getting leads causes sales" or marketing, or phone calls, or good sales techniques. It's easy to be scattered and think that 10 different things cause sales. But you can't focus on 10 different things. Kramers also didn't assume that everyone in the same industry would have the same answer for that question.

There could be many different—but correct—answers. For one company, the answer might be facilitating designs so that they convert into sales more quickly and smoothly. For another, the answer might be how many out-bound phone calls each salesperson makes per day. Or sales might be caused by how many people are selling or how well trained they are. Your answer to "what causes sales" should be one answer and should be the one on which you focus your attention and effort because facilitating that area would have the greatest impact on your sales volume.

"When do I pull the trigger?" is the second question that came out of Kramers' presentation and it has continued to swirl around in my head. Let me back up here and explain. I have always urged our clients to develop a budget for the oncoming year. I tried to emphasize that they should be realistically optimistic. Kramers calls this budget the RBR (realistic but reasonable) budget. He goes farther to recommend a second budget – the BAG (big, audacious goal) budget. By planning with these two budgets, you have created a range and motivated your staff to do more, rather than possibly settle for less. If you hit in that range, you will be happy, and if the BAG is achieved, there will be some very positive and defined incentive that all will receive.

It's especially important that when the economy is uncertain that all our clients actually plan with three budgets. We have added a lower end cut-and-slash budget based on volume that is 30% less than the RBR. This budget inevitably means a serious cut in personnel, so you might want to develop this budget in private and keep it handy in your desk drawer.

Here's where that "when do I pull the trigger?" question comes into play. If you don't accompany this budget with metrics that will trigger the tough decisions that the budget encompasses (for example, moving the office back home, selling two vehicles, cutting one designer and the office assistant, cutting all salaries by 10% and cutting the owner's by 30%), you are likely to delay your decision too long. And you will be overwhelmed emotionally in the heart of the decision-making process. By thinking and planning ahead, you will reinforce the urgency of having an RBR budget and you will make rational decisions about what to do if you have to cut.

Recently, I asked some of our clients what their trigger points are and there was a lot of variation. Here are some of the areas for which they have established metrics:

➤ Budgeted backlog (sold volume not yet built) vs. actual

➤ Monthly dollar volume of estimates vs. target volume

➤ Monthly lead volume vs. target

➤ Monthly sales volume vs. target

➤ Dollar volume in design vs. target

All of these areas are early warning predictors of a slowdown in volume and production. By establishing clear numbers that will trigger your cut-and-slash budget, you will take indecision out of your action. Hopefully you won't need to take these difficult actions. But it has been my perception that one of the biggest mistakes that remodelers have made in downturns is waiting too long to cut. Typically you eat up your cash and work backlog. And that can be fatal.

Put a Little Zingerman's in Your Business

I am fired up! I've been to Ann Arbor, Mich., and it's a neat college town. But the reason I'm fired up is visiting and learning from a fired-up company that's based there. Called "the coolest small company in America" by *Inc.* magazine, Zingerman's Community of Businesses opened up their operations to 90 of our members and we saw an incredibly strong brand in operation, learned how a truly shared vision can power that brand and support it with passion and excellence in execution, and experienced how a company can grow through diversification and shared risk.

First, a caution and a strong opinion. Some remodelers are very linear in thinking and feel that their business learning only comes directly from other remodelers. They are partially right in that we can learn so much from our peers who have already conquered some of the hurdles we face.

But if you want to propel your company forward, if you want to think beyond the edge, if you want to beat tomorrow's competitors before they even arrive, you have to be learning from the very best in whatever industry they exist in. This takes a higher form of thinking because their challenges will not be exactly the same as yours and their solutions must be adapted to our industry. But the payoff can be grand.

Back to Zingerman's, a community of 32 businesses doing $35 million in annual sales selling premium food products in Michigan's doubly recessed economy. They started as a deli and have progressed to mail order, restaurants, a bakery, a creamery, and a training division.

Here are just a few of my takeaways:

They've developed a well-defined philosophical infrastructure that allows them to align all their staff and all their systems and their culture. Their mission, vision, and guiding principles elevate their daily work from drudgery to significance. As the stonemason said (and Zingerman's repeats), "I'm not just laying stone, I'm building a cathedral." And they've made this philosophy very simple and very learnable. This shared philosophy becomes more than critical in aligning 32 businesses, each of which is expected to support the brand.

The training of each employee is paramount. Each carries a paper pocket-sized "passport" with what they need to learn in their job and what they need to learn about Zingerman's. As they learn these elements through formal class or mentoring, they get checked off. This training includes the philosophical differences that support the brand as well as the metrics that support the business plus the learning that each employee needs in their job.

The original business had two partners and, as they add new divisions to their community, it is run under the corporate umbrella by an additional managing partner who might be a long-time employee who has proved their mettle or may be someone new, like a chef. The starting of a new business goes through rigorous vetting and must fit the company's mission and vision. The new partner buys into the new business. This is a business that grows through new ventures that are aligned with the original venture.

There is a triple bottom line and all components get measured. They aspire to great food, great service, and great finance. They are open book but will tolerate the long financial nurturing of individual businesses—provided those businesses still hit the mark on the two remaining bottom lines of food and service. The monitoring of key activities leading to success in each business has been made very simple and is monitored on a daily basis during the morning huddle and posted on a large white board that every staff person can see. These metrics are not static but are changed as needed.

We visited their bakery, creamery, and a restaurant, eating all the way. We questioned lots of staff to see if what we had learned was really in operation, and indeed it was.

I have to end with a personal experience of the Zingerman's difference. During dinner at one of their restaurants, a waitperson named Sharon came by to ask if I was "finished enjoying." What a nice subtlety. Then she asked if I wanted coffee. I said I'd love some decaf but only if she gave me her phone number to call at midnight if I was still awake, because it's not unusual to have regular coffee substituted. She laughed. But soon I was the one laughing because between the coffee cup and the saucer was a napkin with her name and phone number on it. Needless to say, I didn't need it.

Influencing

Looking at the title of the book *Influencer: The Power to Change Anything*, I assumed it would be about developing charisma, great verbal skills, and telling and retelling the vision. Influencing sounds like leading the parade where you want it to go and carrying the banner high.

I was so wrong. Rather, influencing as seen by the authors (Patterson, Grenny, Maxfield, McMillan, and Switzler) is about hard work and about building a very structured program to change behavior. I loved their first book, *Crucial Conversations,* because it made so much sense, was relatively simple in concept, and could be quickly put into use in your business life, your family life, and all aspects of your world.

Perhaps it was myopic to think that developing the ability to "change anything" would be so easily gained. The authors emphasize that becoming an agent of change—an influencer—is based on learning very specific skills and on careful diagnosis of the problem. They also make clear that influence is value neutral and can be used for either good or bad purposes.

As a consultant and meeting facilitator, my work, if successful, is all about changing what company owners do, what goals they set, how they build and motivate a team to achieve those goals, and how they measure success. In other words, I need to be an influencer of company owners who want to become better influencers.

Rather than developing their system for making change from a theoretical perspective, the authors went out and found examples of impossible changes wrought through systematic approaches. They then dissected them to find the strategic and tactical infrastructure that underlay their success.

They examine the Delancey Street Foundation in San Francisco, a conglomerate of several dozen businesses that has mainstreamed 90% of the 14,000 thieves, prostitutes, and murderers it has served into respectability. There is only one professional staff member—the director, Dr. Mimi Silbert. The foundation receives no donations or grants and has no therapists or guards. Then the authors examine how The Carter Center began their assault on Guinea worm disease, which is now eradicated in 11 of the 20 targeted countries. All of their examples are compelling and educational and show progress in changing behaviors that is much more difficult than anything you or I would face.

In each case, success hinged on defining a handful of high-leverage behaviors that, if changed, would topple the problem. They also looked for "positive deviance"—that is, finding examples of success and using them to help define the high-leverage behaviors. How might this apply to your business?

For instance, you could define those few high-leverage behaviors that differentiate your top sales people from those with lackluster performance. You are examining positive deviance. That would allow you to develop a recipe for success in sales in your company. Sample behaviors might be how many first visits were made, how many leads were self generated, the ability to ask for the sale, etc.

Once high-leverage behaviors are isolated and positive deviance studied, the authors identify six sources of influence to change to the desired behaviors; three relate to motivating and three to developing the skills or ability. If I want to lose 20 pounds, I have to be truly motivated and I have to know what behaviors will be successful. If you want your production staff to be more accountable for the gross profit their jobs deliver, you have to define the few behaviors that they need to learn and provide the motivation for them to take the appropriate action.

The three sources of influence for motivating are personal (make the undesirable desirable), social (harness peer pressure), and structural (design rewards and demand accountability). The three that involve developing ability are also personal (surpass your limits), social (find strength in numbers), and structural (change the environment so that the necessary tools are available).

As you can see this is not a quick take, simple premise. But it is well documented and makes clear why so many of our quick-fix changes just are not well conceived and well supported and thus aren't successful. The authors could have made their model easier to comprehend and I wish they had. But the book is well worth reading and taking the time to digest because it is about such a critical subject—change—in our businesses and our lives.

Multitasking to the Max

Betty, the remodeler's office manager, whispered in my ear, "He just can't stay with anything. I've been trying to get him to finish some estimates that might turn into jobs, but he doesn't settle down and do them!" Betty's assessment fit well with some other difficulties I had noticed Jim, the remodeler, having as I evaluated his company.

"Jim, I'm certainly not a doctor," I said, "but have you ever been tested for attention deficit disorder (ADD)?" With that, Jim pulled a vial of pills of the most common ADD medicine out of his desk drawer. We then moved on to how he might manage this challenge to do the quiet, settled work that every remodeler must do.

Since that epiphany 10 years ago, I have found that two or three clients that I work with each year exhibit the signs of ADD—distractibility, impulsivity, and restlessness. The remodeling business is so full of different roles, different jobsites, and different crises that it gives even ardent multi-taskers a challenge. It is an attractive business for those who are distractible, impulsive, and restless! If these descriptions fit you, you might want to do some "Googling" to research ADD.

But now a prominent psychiatrist has written in a highly respected business journal that we can create a similar syndrome to ADD in ourselves and in those who work for us. In the January, 2005 *Harvard Business Review*, Edward Hallowell, M.D., describes what happens to our brains when we try to do too much too quickly. He notes, "Everywhere people rely on their cell phones, e-mail, and digital assistants in the race to gather and transmit data, plans, and ideas faster and faster." In his article entitled "Why Smart People Underperform," Hallowell describes how our demanding jobs can lead to overloaded circuits and ADT, or attention deficit trait.

While Hallowell defines ADD as a "neurological disorder that has a genetic component and can be aggravated by environmental and physical factors," ADT springs entirely from the environment. In other words, we bring it on ourselves by multitasking to the max. In fact, you may be reading this column while otherwise occupied. It is a response to our hyperkinetic environment— often self-induced.

The core symptoms of ADT are described as distractibility, inner frenzy, and impatience. Sound familiar? "People with ADT have difficulty staying organized, setting priorities, and managing time," says the author.

But what to do? Hallowell recommends those old standbys like eating well, getting enough sleep, exercising at least 30 minutes every other day, and taking vitamins. For work, he gives 12 tips for breaking the brain overload. Here are the first three:

➤ Do all you can to create a trusting, connected work environment.

➤ Have a friendly, face-to-face talk with a person you like every 4 to 6 hours.

➤ Break large tasks into smaller ones.

Feeling overwhelmed? Here are Hallowell's four recommendations based on reordering brain function:

➤ Slow down.

➤ Do an easy rote task.

➤ Move around: Go up and down a flight of stairs or walk briskly.

➤ Ask for help, delegate a task, or brainstorm with a colleague. In short, do not worry alone.

Note that these recommendations do not include grinning and bearing it, yelling at staff, plowing on bravely, or kicking the dog.

Pillow Talk

There's nothing like holidays to remind us how wonderful and how imperfect our families are, so it seems appropriate to talk about spouses working together. Much of this applies also to other family members in your business as well.

Remodeling is full of businesses where both spouses work side by side. I've consulted with many companies where spouses working together have been a great asset but I've also seen many heart-rending situations where couples are putting their marriages in serious jeopardy. Here are eight tips that will help you get on the right footing.

Settle the business hierarchy.

Are you partners or is there an owner/employee relationship? This needs to be an up-front conversation. Is your spouse working to help you or working because they are passionate about it? Are they willing to put their dreams aside to assist you temporarily or do they want to be an equal partner? Once decided, this needs to be clearly communicated to your staff.

Clarify whether your marriage is more important than the business.

If so, it may mean that if you can't work out a healthy business relationship, one of you will go elsewhere to protect the marriage.

Leave family outside the business door.

The carping or screaming matches you have at home are not appropriate at work. Stay professional and model professional behavior to the staff.

Leave business outside the family door.

Create sacrosanct ground rules as to whether the business can be discussed at home and under what circumstances. Many dysfunctional spouses leave the office but never leave the business.

Work for common goals.

Don't be competitive with one another because both of you are sailing in the same boat. It's either win-win or lose-lose. This agreement on the big picture will help you ride out smaller disagreements.

Create separate turf.

If each of you have your own part of the business pie, then you are less likely to cross swords. When in doubt defer to the "owner" of that area.

Be sure both of you are paid at least market rate for the job you do. That equity tends to settle a lot of potential grievances before they develop.

Meet formally.

Especially if you are partners, don't depend on passing conversations to handle all issues. Create a weekly partners meeting with a standing agenda to which any special items can be added. If it is an owner/employee relationship, then the employee spouse would meet as appropriate for an outside employee.

I have a pet peeve and hope you'll join me in ridding the business world of an insidious phrase. Let's ban the oft-used and demeaning term "mom and pop" business. Two unified partners working with a shared vision toward common goals in a professional manner is a superb business asset. We should all be so lucky.

Passing On

There is nothing more beautiful than the successful transfer of a family-owned remodeling company to the second generation. But oh—the many heart-breaking stories that lie behind some of these transfers. So if you are in the midst or hope to have a family member buy and take over your company in the future, learn from the experts and those who've walked this stony path.

As a consultant, I've visited companies where the upcoming-but-not-yet owners were tyrants with staff and took every advantage of their positions with the tacit permission of their parent(s). More commonly, in other companies, I've interviewed each generation separately, only to find what they thought was going to happen and when they thought it would happen was a total mismatch. More times than I can count, I've seen second generation owners-to-be waiting patiently for a parent to give clear indication of when they would be leaving and what skills the second generation must exhibit before taking over.

Surveys show that only 30% of family firms successfully transfer to the second generation and only 10% make it to the third generation. Here are some thoughts based on my experiences and on interviewing some great second generation owners.

➤ Allow enough time. Once you and your son or daughter have decided to pursue this path, think in terms of a 3-to-5-year timeline.

➤ Seek long-term outside help from a family business specialist. Abe Degnan of Degnan Design Builders Inc., in DeForest, Wisc., has been through this journey in taking over the company from his dad and says his best piece of advice is to "work with several trusted advisors like an accountant, attorney, and mediator or coach." Degnan notes that really four people were involved (himself, his dad, and both spouses) and that navigating the business/personal interactions is complex.

➤ Develop a path with defined skills and milestones that must be learned by the daughter or son to safeguard the successful transfer.

➤ The better systematized and the better staffed your company is, the safer the transfer will be. Annette Parrish, who along with her husband, Larry, purchased Parrish Construction Company in Boulder, Colo., from his dad, notes that although the transition was smooth, "it would have been much smoother if we had had written procedures and documentation of the first 20 years of the company," says Annette.

➤ Have a written succession plan. How will the company be valued and how will that value be transferred? When will the transfer occur? How and when will the first generation exit? What role(s) will they play until then?

➤ One of the best avenues to train the second generation is to put them in a peer group like our Remodelers Advantage Roundtables and let them represent the company. In order to do this, they may need to have some ownership percentage and if they make commitments, they need to be able to fulfill them. They will learn to read financials, hear stories of success and failure, develop their own group of mentors, and generally begin thinking like a CEO.

➤ And when the time comes, the founder needs to let go and let the next generation fly. They will have new ideas and they will want change. In the best of all worlds, the values of the first generation will endure but the business will evolve to meet the new realities of a new owner and a new world.

Paul Karofsky, Ed.M, director of the Family Business Center at Northeastern University, puts perspective on this transfer of the business legacy. He says, "The successful perpetuation of your family business just may be the closest you will ever come to immortality."

Help is Only a Consultant Away

You are in a quandary. Maybe you've poured your heart and soul (and sweat and tears) into your company with only a meager return. Or your daughter has come on board with the intent of owning the business in just a few years but the two of you just aren't seeing eye to eye. Perhaps you feel that a lack of systems and processes is holding you back. Or you just aren't sure what position should be filled next. The list of business challenges can be endless.

You've exhausted all the potential solutions you know about. You've read the magazines, bought the books, and tried talking to your peers at the remodeling association. You are stumped. It may be time to bring in an outside consultant or business coach. First, stop and think about how you would answer these questions:

Do you want a consultant or a coach?
While these terms are used somewhat interchangeably, there is a difference. A coach asks questions and helps you find the answer within yourself. A consultant is an expert who brings a menu of solutions and works with you to choose the best one for you. A consultant is more authoritative and directive than a coach. These terms are often confused even by the practitioners, so you should ask about them as you interview prospective candidates. For the purposes of this column, I'll use the terms interchangeably.

Do you want a candidate whose expertise is industry-specific or who works with different types of businesses in different industries?
For financial issues, you might well prefer someone who knows how successful remodelers operate financially and has a clear understanding of the common financial benchmarks and preferred method of accounting. On the other hand, if you are having a family business problem, you would do well to choose a consultant in that area who undoubtedly works in many different industries because the family dynamics issues are similar. In marketing, estimating, and production, industry-specific wins. In sales, you might find a sales specialist is your preference and industry is less important.

Do you want a consultant to help you think through the issues or implement the solution or both?

Your investment creeps in here in that the former tends to be more expensive but requires much less time in your company. Implementers tend to be less expensive but have a much longer term contract. Everyone dreams of the "magic" solution—the change-one-thing-and-everything-will-work answer. Unfortunately, magic rarely (I mean really *rarely*) exists. Implementation is hard work but really important work. It's my opinion that the company needs to learn to implement internally. The consultant may need to teach you to fish but not provide your dinner.

What is your budget?

This is a tough one to answer and relates in part to whether the consultant/coach is local or from out of town. You may not always have a choice to go local but usually, if the candidate fits, it is much less expensive to have a local expert. If they are from afar, you'll need to figure their fee plus hotel, meals, and travel expenses. Fees could be all over the board and will relate to the length of the contract, but I will make a stab here. Figure $2,000 to $6,000 a day for a short, strategic assessment of your company that includes agreed-upon deliverables. While the fee sounds steep, the actual time spent at the company will undoubtedly be augmented by gathering information from you upfront, planning an efficient agenda onsite, and following up with a written report.

Do you want on-site consulting or telephonic consulting?

While consulting by telephone may sound strange, it actually works—especially for clearly defined issues. Frequency could be weekly or bi-weekly or monthly and should include "homework" to be done between each call. These regular check-ins can take a problem and break it into manageable bites. They also break the fees into more manageable payments. You might explore this avenue.

Is there any guarantee that you will be satisfied?

Ask about this. Confident consultants with successful formats may well refund your fees if you are not satisfied at some early stage. This can make you feel more confident and reduce the risk of creating the relationship.

A last caveat: Choose a consultant who will work themselves out of a job, not into a job. You want someone who will teach you and your organization to be independent of them, not make you dependent on continuing services.

And a last encouragement: Sometimes, paying a hired gun is ultimately what gets you to pay attention and take action. Frequently, hiring the right consultant can enable you to bypass that old "reinventing the wheel" and save years in developing your company.

Business Straight to the Heart

chapter two

LEARNING AND
EARNING LEADERSHIP

Leadership Pure and Simple

Leadership Hurdles

Six Leadership Habits

Volunteer Employees

Glorious Execution

Success to Significance

Finding the North Star

Glue that Creates Greatness

Culture Immersion

"Management is efficiency in climbing the ladder of success; leadership determines whether the ladder is leaning against the right wall."

Stephen R. Covey

L EADERSHIP IS ONE OF THOSE FAMILIAR WORDS. We use it all the time. We assume we know what it means and that others do, too. We know it's vital to getting things done but if asked to define it, we can stumble.

What does leadership look like? Some leaders are humble. Some leaders are great salespeople with plenty of self confidence. But somehow, no matter what their style is, true leaders inspire others to embrace their vision and goals.

How many leaders are there? Really, there's the potential for every human to be a leader in some sphere, whether it be church or school or county or chess club. Our job as business people is to be both a leader and a grower of leaders. What if you focused on creating leadership at every level in your company? What would be the benefit? You'd have happier staff and they would take more off your shoulders. That's a pretty good deal.

Leadership Pure and Simple

Has there ever been a greater need for leadership—for our country, our states, and our companies? Your staff is worried and your potential clients are worried, as are your vendors and trade contractors. A leader is someone we look to when we feel lost. They reenergize us and give us direction. If they are feeling lost as well, they mask it and dig in. Some of us may think we are leaders and others may not be so sure. So what does it take to be a leader?

If you Google the term, you'll get close to 1.5 million citations. But can it be that difficult? That mysterious? We think we know leaders when we see them, yet we know people who firmly believe in a leader (for instance, in a cult) that we don't believe in at all. So let's try to define some of the qualities that reinforce leadership in a remodeler or a lead carpenter or a trade contractor.

Peter Drucker, the business management guru, lists three key qualities that every leader shares. He points out that they must be accompanied by consistency and hard work:

1. *The ability to build and articulate a vision that others want to achieve.* If you want to strengthen this area, you'll want to engage your staff in developing a written vision, mission, and core values statement and then help make those ideals real and alive in the company through their constant communication and use. Everyone wants their daily work to be part of something bigger than they are—something grander, something significant.

2. *The acceptance of leadership as a responsibility, not a rank.* In fact, you'll want to find and nurture this precious ability anywhere and everywhere on the organizational chart. You'll want to constantly develop leadership in your staff through developing the company culture, training, and delegating responsibility. And it means letting good folks fail when the consequences are not too severe. After all, that's how we learned.

3. *The ability to earn and keep trust.* Why do we trust someone? Because they deliver on their promises even when it's hard and the cost is high. We can count on them. They have our back. We want to model the values and behaviors we want in our staff. We want to take responsibility

for our mistakes, thereby creating a safe environment for others to do so.

To Drucker's wisdom, let me dare to add a few more that I have observed in great remodelers:

Leadership is often associated with *change* because leaders establish a company's direction and motivate staff to believe in and follow that direction. I can't think of a time when this has been more important. If you are faced with downsizing, for instance, you juggle job assignments, take pay cuts, and your staff has to believe in you and your plan. You have to find and "sell" the "pony in the manure pile."

And that leads directly to the ability of a leader to make the *tough choices*—to fire, to downsize, to change direction when necessary for the health of the company. Over the last few years, you have probably been making those tough choices—hopefully with a minimum of procrastination and always communicating them in the context of the bigger picture.

Leaders drive *continuous improvement* in the company. In order to develop strong leaders, accurate information is shared with staff so they, too, can be strong leaders making sound suggestions and decisions. Even in these tough times, this means we must allot enough time for our staff to work ON the company, not just IN the company. We allot that time to ourselves and staff knowing that it will return substantial benefit and is the only way to ensure consistent company success.

So if you own the company or are a carpenter or a designer or an office manager, you have the ability to be a leader. Nothing on the list is impossible, yet we all probably have at least a little work we can do to shape up. If you focus on improving these six areas you'll be amazed how many folks will fall in with you and help you achieve your significant vision.

Leadership Hurdles

The next year is right around the corner. Will you be planning some growth for your company? Will you be planning some growth for yourself and your leadership skills? Entrepreneurs often underestimate—or totally overlook—the challenges that growth will place on their leadership and management skills. Just as the company will be undergoing major upheavals as it grows, you will be changing your relationship to the company. Many of the traits and talents that served you so well in a smaller company will become hurdles to be overcome.

John Hamm writes about this in his article, *"Why Entrepreneurs Don't Scale,"* in the *Harvard Business Review* (9/02). He notes, "A leader who scales is able to jettison habits and skills that have outlived their usefulness and adapt to new challenges along the way."

Hamm identifies four tendencies that work at some stage for business leaders but become "Achilles' heels" or weak spots as the company grows:

A tendency toward *loyalty* to comrades, those who were there from the beginning or who lived through tough times, even when those comrades are giving signs of failure or an inability to keep up with the changes that growth demands. Hamm calls this failure on a leader's part to grow with the company "stubborn loyalty, at the expense of an organization's success," and notes that it is extremely common in growing companies. I heartily concur. The remodeler must make some tough decisions as to who has the skills to take the company to the next level and who doesn't. Some who can do their present jobs well will stay but not progress to new levels of management. Others, even though they are liked and respected and cared about, will have to leave for other opportunities.

A tendency to *task orientation,* or focusing on the job at hand. In other words, leaders who fail to become more strategic end up with an ever-growing to-do list and a blurring of priorities. "Leaders able to scale…learn to extract three or four high-level goals …and focus their teams…" notes Hamm.

There are remodelers who own $3 million dollar companies and report spending 2 hours a week working *on* the company (as differentiated from *in* the company). This simply won't fly. Bigger companies need—demand—management and leadership time that only an owner can provide. They call out for a strategic vision and direction against which every activity is measured. There are systemic problems, people problems, and economic problems. As a company grows, risk grows and the remodeler has to be reading the vital signs and motivating folks to move in the right direction. A few hours a week as a company grows to multi-million dollar volume simply won't do it.

A tendency to be *single-minded,* which can turn into tunnel vision as the company grows. The owner of a growing company is much like the clown who has to keep many plates spinning in the air. They can't focus just on sales or just on estimating; there are many endeavors that must be recognized, acknowledged, and prioritized.

A tendency to *work in isolation.* This trait can be powerful in an entrepreneur and disastrous in leading a larger company with an increasing number of stakeholders. There are a growing number of employees and clients and subs and suppliers and a leader. Without losing sight of the priorities, the remodeler has to be in the right place with the right person at the right time. This takes new skills and personal growth.

These four tendencies of an entrepreneur work for a small start-up company but restrict the growth and success of a larger enterprise. As Hamm notes, leaders who grow "make concerted, sometimes uncomfortable efforts to do what doesn't come naturally to them for the team's sake."

So as you plan and look at what might be required to grow your company, don't forget to include yourself and your skills in the decision.

The Six Habits

It might be called the "Six Habits of Highly Successful Leaders." Yes, I know Stephen Covey stole and adapted my title before I ever thought of it. Covey's long-time bestseller is *The Seven Habits of Highly Effective People*. Not to worry; it's the wisdom within the concepts that count.

For years, my partner Victoria Downing and I have worked to distill the key business habits that make for success among our remodeler clients. It is still a work in progress, but see what you think. We've visualized our Success System as a pyramid. The habits are prioritized from bottom to top. In other words, the lowest item has the highest priority.

HABIT ONE: Sound Financial Management. Money is the bedrock a company is built on. Without money, none of the rest matters. It fuels your ability to stay in business, satisfy clients, and keep contented staff. And you only know where your money is and whether you have any through accurate reporting that directs the way to sound management decisions.

Right now, I am trying to work with a company owner who is drowning in debt. That would be bad enough but his books are virtually non-existent and with no money to pay someone to get them right, we are flying blind. Is he charging the right price? Probably not, but we really don't know. Is he selling the right number of jobs, the right kind of jobs? Tracking money in a $500,000 or $5,000,000 remodeling company involves lots of time and money but without that information, nothing else matters.

HABIT TWO: Efficient Organizational Structure. The majority of remodeling companies start with an owner who does everything and then begins to hire field staff and perhaps an office person. It's a pretty simple organization and doesn't require much thought on how work is distributed and who's responsible for what. But to grow to having 20 or 40 or 60 people on staff and to have your company running smoothly, you need to have thought out how you want to organize your "departments"—admin, sales, production, design, estimating, marketing, etc. How does the responsibility and accountability for making the company successful distribute in your company? In most companies, unfortunately, it all falls on the owner. We need to change that.

HABIT THREE: Effective Team Building. This is a really big area and trips up many a remodeler. While staffing a company with "A" players is harder than ever before, most of us simply do not give it the time and effort it demands. We hire the best of the available and then they sink or swim without a job description or a policy manual or training or coaching. I could go on and on here, but I bet you know what I mean.

This area includes retaining key employees and motivating them to do their best and to take responsibility for seeing that the right things happen in their area of influence. Business is a team sport that demands harnessing individuals into a team that acts for the common good. Out of that comes your team working together to produce delighted clients while obtaining the right gross profit for the business.

HABIT FOUR: Strong Leadership. This area works hand-in-hand with Effective Team Building. Great teams need—and demand—great leaders. Most of us have a mental picture of what an outstanding leader should "look" like. And inevitably we underestimate our ability to lead. But I've seen great leadership from all types of personalities—from quiet to charismatic. Great leaders create a magnetic vision that draws and invites staff to participate with passion.

HABIT FIVE: Enhanced Company Culture. All remodeling companies have an underlying culture that in smaller companies results from the owner's philosophy of how people (clients, staff) should be treated and the environment in which they should work. As a remodeler grows, that culture will be taken over by strong (but not necessarily good) natural leaders in the company. A smart owner knows that to have the unique company that only they can create, they must define, control, grow, and monitor their magnetic culture. An outstanding company culture transforms a successful company into a significant company.

And running concurrently with all five of the above habits is **HABIT SIX: Well Developed Systems.** All successful companies make success predictable through providing proven systems that help individual team members avoid errors and enhance client satisfaction. In all your operational areas such as estimating or design or sales, your company's way of doing business should be defined, taught, and preserved until change is due. How can a company deliver predictable excellence if each employee is doing it their own way?

These six key habits are prioritized like a ladder. If you haven't mastered habit one (financial), focus there first. The successful company is undoubtedly working in all areas all the time, but to have a strong foundation your company and you must master each habit before making the next habit your major focus.

Creating Volunteer Employees

At a recent Remodelers Advantage Roundtables meeting that I facilitated, 12 highly successful remodelers were discussing how they could hone their leadership skills. I asked each attendee to think of a time when they felt they were at their personal best as a leader. Then each in turn related their story. Surprise! None were business related. Almost all involved volunteer work in a charity or community project or association.

We decided that a volunteer project has the following components:
> a clear start and finish
> a clear objective
> an easy way to measure success
> volunteer workers. Because the workers were volunteers, they had to be motivated and infused with a shared vision by the leader.

The consensus was that business is like parenting in that it is ever-ongoing and often doesn't have distinct stop and start points. Indeed, work may not inspire a shared vision and many times those employees sure don't seem like volunteers.

Yet, couldn't we add these ingredients to our business? Each job can be looked at as a "project" with a clear beginning and end and a schedule that documents and improves on that flow. Each job has a clear objective—on time and on budget with a delighted client. We can measure all three of these things and share our findings.

Or we can work "on" the company in bite size pieces—for instance, taking on the project of cleaning up the sales-to-production handoff and that can be our project. Our goal might be to run one job completely by the system we've created to make sure it works before we apply it to all jobs. Almost every important task can be broken down into discrete component parts and success can be defined and celebrated.

Now we get to the hard one—volunteers. Let me share an example from this meeting. One member—we'll name him Gene—posted his large company's organizational chart, which showed virtually everyone in the office reporting to him. Then, as he discussed the challenges he was dealing with, Gene kept referring to what employees wouldn't do, couldn't do, and didn't like to do. Every employee seemed to be a prima donna who needed special care. All the loose ends fell to Gene to do and the overload was burning him out.

Two company owners helped Gene out with sage advice. Both of them have clear policies that every employee must *want to work* for the company. If you want to work for a company as a base requirement to your employment, you are ready to accept the job descriptions and policies of that company. If you don't like those, you won't want to work for the company and will move on. As owner, you may like an employee, even love an employee and you may value their talent and expertise highly. But if they don't really care whether they work for you or not, they need to be somewhere else.

You might say, "Of course everyone here wants to work for my company. They're here aren't they?" We all have dealt with employees of service companies that don't seem to want to work there, so don't underestimate this concept. It frees you as employer although it certainly behooves every company owner to create a fun, enthusiastic, and excellent company that many people would want to work for. That gives the owner many potential employees to choose from. This concept creates a base from which you can insist that the rules, procedures, and systems will be followed.

But once you have "volunteers" in your company, you must—as leader—fire them up with that inspired vision. They want to know where the company is going, where their job is going, and what constitutes success in the small picture and in the big picture. And they want to have fun getting there. It's simple, but it sure isn't easy.

Glorious Execution

So where are those copious notes you took during last year's Remodeling Show? Or the neat sales-to-production-handoff form you got from your remodeler buddy that you wanted to adapt and begin using? And then you bought a book on how to put the lead carpenter system into place because you were determined that this would be the year you accomplished this transition. But where is it now? Have you opened it yet? We won't even go into the now-out-of-date software you have purchased that hasn't been installed yet.

I used to think that giving birth to an idea, a system, or a way to make things better was the highest achievement a businessperson could make. Now I know much better. It is the successful *execution* of that idea that takes considerably longer and requires constant monitoring until it is a habit; that isn't quite as zingy, but that is the true achievement.

As I work with remodeling companies, I frequently find a lack of execution— of failed implementation. The owner decrees that from now on everyone will turn in their time cards in a certain way and at a certain time. But each field person responds in their own way until the decree has vanished into thin air. One good idea after another goes up in smoke.

So I was intrigued by the book, *Execution: The Discipline of Getting Things Done,* by Larry Bossidy and Ram Charan. *Business Week* called it a "how-to book for the can-do boss," which was a compelling recommendation since remodelers are can-do above all else. The authors define execution as the missing link between "what a company's leaders want to achieve and the ability of their organizations to deliver it."

Bossidy and Charan very quickly clear up the myth that leadership involves thinking rather than doing. They designate execution as the leader's most important work. To get ideas into implementation, the business leader must combine clear communication, accountability for results, and constant follow-through to ensure plans are on track. Most importantly, the doers in an organization need to be rewarded and promoted.

They note, "The failure to follow through is widespread in business, and a major cause of poor execution. How many meetings have you attended where people left without firm conclusions about who would do what and when? Everybody may have agreed the idea was good, but since nobody was named accountable for results, it doesn't get done."

Here are my five simple recommendations to help with execution. Consistency here will develop a discipline of execution in your company over the next 6 to 12 months.

- ➤ Start with small bites. It is better to succeed at something small than fail at something big. You can eat an elephant (should you desire to) one bite at a time.
- ➤ Assign accountability for follow-through to a person or a team. Pick people who are enthusiastic and would be positively affected by the outcome.
- ➤ Always designate who will do what by when and follow up.
- ➤ Reward those who get things done. Get rid of those who don't. (I could say "execute" them, but I won't). Start today.
- ➤ Execution needs to become a company habit. And habits take time. Let's say your bookkeeper is having trouble getting the time cards submitted on time and with accurate information. This might be your approach: Task the field, any production supervisors, and your bookkeeper to meet and work together to assess where the hurdles are and how to solve them.

This will also act to educate each person about the others' needs and get buy-in. Maybe they develop a mini-game for the next four weeks that if every time card is submitted on time, there is a reward for that week (the boss will hand deliver donuts and coffee to the job site for 1 week's reward, for instance.) This creates peer pressure on every worker to not let the team down. The production manager is the point person who will remind and cajole and even chastise if needed. Four weeks of making this a habit and working out any kinks should solve the problem and is enough time to begin making it a habit.

Ongoing successful execution is the ultimate achievement in any company.

Success to Significance

Vision. Mission. Purpose. Culture. Core Values. Do you ever find these concepts fuzzy, overlapping, and a little hard to grasp? If so, you are in very good company. You might also question whether they even belong in a small entrepreneurial business. Or you might wonder if time spent thinking about them and work spent defining them might just be for marketing specialists who only want to use them in the company's ads.

Each expert seems to have their own take on what is and isn't important about these concepts, but there is no argument about their link to a significant business. Most of us are jaundiced consumers about companies that splash their mission statement about. And our company meeting time is so precious and so expensive that devoting it to the impractical or too theoretical is to rob the client or the project at hand.

If you have six draft horses and want to plow a field, would the time spent harnessing those horses be a waste? Of course not, because that would be the way you would turn them into a team. You would be able to control their direction and maximize their output.

Employees are certainly not horses, but purpose, culture, core values, vision are all the ways that you help your team to pull together, to make effective decisions, and to work with the true end in mind.

Let me recommend a really good book. It's easy to read—actually the story of how two people in an insurance company define the company's purpose, core values, and vision. And along the way, they apply these concepts to a school and to one of their families.

The book is *Full Steam Ahead,* by Ken Blanchard and Jesse Stoner. If you would like people to not just work at your company but to work even more effectively and be attracted and nurtured by your values, you need to define and disseminate your culture. If you would like them to focus on a larger purpose, to see a significance to their work beyond the day-to-day, this book is a really helpful resource.

As an owner you have a vision for your company, but is it compelling to others? Your company already has a culture—it's what one employee tells their brother who is interested in working for you. It's the underground "skinny" on the company. It may be good, it may be bad. It's likely to be a mix. And you certainly have core values. They may include greed or generosity, respect or lack thereof, or you may treat clients one way and employees another. Those core values will usually come from the owner. But when they are not openly defined, a strong employee may be setting up their own culture and values and those may be toxic to yours. You want to manage your culture and you want it to be positive and inspiring.

Exceptional companies should bring their positive culture and values to the surface. Then they can be openly lived, discussed, measured, and taught. They can be powerful in attracting like-thinking new hires and in retaining your existing staff. Defined guidelines as to how your company does business will make many tough decisions much easier.

Southwest Airlines, Walmart, Disney, L.L. Bean, and Ritz-Carlton are exceptional companies that believed that in order to rise from competency to mastery they needed a team that clearly knew and believed in the company "way."

How could you even begin this journey? Look at it as having two phases—the definition phase and the living-it phase. If you haven't defined your company's purpose, mission, vision, and values and delved into the congruent behaviors that accompany them, that will be phase one.

Start by getting each of your employees their own copy of *Full Steam Ahead*. Then hold discussions around the book whether in full company meetings or by departments. Get the buzz going and decide how you want to proceed. You might bring in a facilitator to help you with an all-day meeting, or you may decide to bootstrap the effort and do it yourself in small chunks.

It has been my experience that most (not all) employees dig right in and are so enthusiastic about this effort because we all want significance in our lives. We want to work for a bigger purpose. We want to see our jobs as important. We want fair and caring rules about how we treat our co-workers and our clients.

And what are mission, purpose, vision, values, and culture? Why, they're the pavers on the road from success to significance.

Finding the North Star

Since I own some stock, my recent mail has brought a spate of annual reports. Usually they are recycled unopened. One year I thought I'd take a quick look. The first one from Dun and Bradstreet led boldly with the company vision on the cover—"To be the most trusted source of business insight so our customers can decide with confidence."

Next in the D&B annual report came a list of the company values and the note that "all our activities and decisions must be based on, and guided by, our values." Here are three from their list of six:

➤ "Treat all people with respect and dignity; value differences."

➤ "Conduct ourselves with the highest level of integrity and business ethics."

➤ "Place the interest of customers first; our success depends on their success."

The list ends with this statement: "By behaving in accordance with these values, we will provide outstanding service to our customers, maintain a leadership position in our business, improve satisfaction for our team members, and provide superior value to our shareholders."

Experts seem to agree that a business driven by an inspiring vision and/or mission and emphasizing core values creates a special workplace where motivated employees can deliver exceptional service to clients. I have found this to be true in my work with remodelers. So I was sure that as the annual reports rolled in, I would find more and more information on how each company pictured itself and on the core values that it taught and guarded and by which it worked. While I had no way to judge whether they truly lived these statements, proclaiming them importantly in telling the company story certainly was a great start.

Here's how the 10 annual reports I received stacked up in communicating the big picture of what the company was about and what rules they would use to play the game of business. No others were as upfront as D&B. In six you could thumb through and find some information about values and culture and vision. In four there was a disappointing and total lack of inspiration and information (other than technical) about where the company was going and what ground rules would guide it in getting there.

That puts Tom Mitchell, owner of Mitchell Construction Inc., in Medfield, Mass., far ahead of these major international corporations. He's investing considerable time and money to develop a clear mission statement and define the core values and behaviors his company will work by. Why? As a member of the Remodelers Advantage Roundtables, "I attended a Disney Institute seminar in Orlando and experienced the effect of a positive culture there," Mitchell says. "I intuitively knew that if my company could offer such a positive culture, there was no way we wouldn't be successful. If we had thrilled employees serving thrilled clients, we would have a personal advantage and a competitive advantage."

Mitchell began by having everyone in the company read *Full Steam Ahead* by Ken Blanchard and Jesse Stoner, which teaches creating a successful vision and defining core values within an engaging story format. Then he brought in a consultant for a full day of interactive defining of the company's vision and values by all staff. That got full buy-in from his staff. Everyone wanted to work under and be part of the defined values and culture they had helped to develop.

Next, Mitchell Construction wrote a charter that named a "Framers Committee" to edit and publish the mission and values statements. "The key people have become enthusiastic," says Mitchell, "and it's their job to keep the rest of the company fired up about culture. We aren't rushing—both because we are busy, and because this is so important. This is forever. We talk about culture every day in every meeting," he says.

Ask Tom Mitchell for some advice for other remodelers who want to start down this culture-initiative path and here's what he says. "You first have to trust that if you make the leap, that it has value. It's not a pep talk. It's the difference between giving a person a fish versus teaching them how to fish. The key is not the end result of having it all on paper; it's the thinking behind that paper that's important. The power isn't in perfecting your company culture—it's in working toward it."

Investing in the Glue that Makes a Great Company

Once upon a time I thought culture meant opera and ballet and classical music. I also knew it was a word used to describe the differences between natives of different countries. I had no idea that I would spend later years working to develop positive company environments—also called cultures.

I am now a convert and like all converts I am missionary in my zeal. A tangible, inspiring, and managed culture is what separates the exceptional companies from the merely good ones. It is what turns success to significance. It can be difficult to get the initiative going and once undertaken, honing your company culture is a forever project. It takes time, money, and focus. It can't be faked and be successful. Here's how one remodeler has begun his company's journey.

Laverne Brubacher, owner of Menno S. Martin Contractor in Ontario, Canada, knew that defining and developing his company's already positive culture into words and actions was an important step toward freeing himself from making daily judgment calls while continuing and enhancing exceptional service delivery. As a well-run remodeling firm, Menno S. Martin had the systems to guide their employees in handling the routine challenges of their work. But those systems only go so far. Good judgment aligned with the company's vision, mission, and core values would be needed to make the many, often tough decisions that were non-routine.

Brubacher brought in a local outside facilitator who set up three major activities. The first was a full-day meeting with Brubacher and his two key managers to draft mission and vision statements. Then they met with everyone in the company—didn't show them the work they had done but got their input. Out of this came their vision ("We will be responsive, innovative, trusted, and caring renovators"), mission ("We design and build comprehensive renovation solutions"), and values (integrity, stewardship, care, team play, and encouragement).

They then met with the entire company to present what they had developed. "These were very aligned with the discussions and recommendations of all our staff, so there was buy-in," says Brubacher. Now it was time to move on to the day-to-day applications of their culture—how they would live and work their beliefs.

"We focused on some of the dos and don'ts of our daily work," says Brubacher. "We got great answers to some key questions like, How do we want the company to be known? What do we want our clients to say about us? What can we do to improve our profitability? What could we do better? As you think of working at Menno S. Martin, what is most important to you about working here?"

Brubacher has invested $15,000 to $20,000 in time and money to date and is enthusiastic about where the culture path is taking the company and the benefits it will yield for both the company and for himself as owner. That path should lead to an exceptional values-based working environment for his personnel and exceptional service delivery for his client.

And that is a significant accomplishment indeed.

Culture Immersion

"How in the world did they do it? We were only there a week and they got us totally into doing it their way—and loving it," my old college chum Ann wondered as we retraced our travel on I-81. We were headed home from the John C. Campbell Folk School in tiny Brasstown, N.C. In addition to learning a craft, my friend and I had just experienced a lesson in culture immersion that could have taught any management guru a thing or two.

Every institution—including your business, your family, your church, your volunteer fire department, and your garden club—has a culture. Usually we learn it by watching, reading between the lines, and deciding what will make us successful or what will get us attention in that environment. Often we do it by stubbing our toe and hearing, "We don't do it that way here." Unlike every small appliance we buy, there is no video and no manual.

If you are a remodeler who would like your life and business philosophy to be seamless, if you would like to create a positive environment at your company that helps people to be their best and to see their work as part of something more significant than just the estimating or designing or carpentering they do, you may want to take a few lessons from this folk school, or Southwest Airlines, or other fine companies that have committed to being more proactive about building a positive culture.

"What, we have to make our own beds?" I said as Ann and I surveyed our rustic accommodations. It was the beginning of an immersion that clearly signified we would be taken care of but not pampered. We did the bed thing and hurried over to the opening orientation with 130 other eager students who were taking classes in everything from blacksmithing to making kaleidoscopes to constructing intricate chocolate boxes.

We learned the school was based on a Danish model where competition was verboten. There would be no grades, no signs that anyone was pursuing anything but the best they could do. Craft would be sacred. Work would be valued. We would come to appreciate the individual journey each student was on.

Mealtime was communal, with tables of eight and healthy food served family style. At orientation we were reminded that much of the learning would come from meeting as many of the other students as possible, so Ann and I circulated independently.

Meals were signaled by a bell and all were expected to hurry into the dining hall, stand behind their chair, pull out a yellow laminated card of non-denominational blessings, and wait for the announcer to lead us in a blessing. Only then would we sit down and pass the food. Dirty dishes and leftovers were to be delivered to different windows by those at the table. An iron fork or spoon displayed beside one window would tell us which utensil to keep for dessert and one table member would pick up the tray of eight desserts to bring back to the table. But I am telling you only a tiny scrap of all the ways we were helped to quickly "get it" and get with it.

Here's the point: This institution runs to its own heartfelt philosophy and ways of doing things and often there is a point to be made, a lesson to be learned from the way things are done. Within a few hours, we who had come from all over the United States, from a competitive dog-eat-dog world that often devalues the work of human hands, had been shaped up to a fare-thee-well.

It had been done so successfully because the school had defined, down to the smallest detail, the experience they wanted us to have, had communicated it very clearly upfront, had aligned hundreds of bits of behavior and procedure to their philosophy, and had given us such a sense of the legacy it represented that we wanted to be part of it. The final result had left us feeling we were making the world a better place. What a wonderful opportunity we leaders have to do this in our own businesses!

chapter three

BUILDING A GREAT TEAM

Play Pro Ball

Home Schooling

Getting the Right Fit

Banish Dysfunction

Misery or Ministry?

Bedrock and Boundaries

Increasing Hiring Wins

The Power of Group Thinking

Freeing Up a Future

Membership in Your Company

Accentuate the Positive

Systematic Disney

Vitamin P

Spreading Good Cheer

Guard Those Systems

Brainstorming

Role Playing

51-Percenters

A Dream With a Date Attached

Gifts to Give All Year

> *"Organization doesn't really accomplish anything. Plans don't accomplish anything, either. Theories of management don't much matter.*
>
> *Endeavors succeed or fail because of the people involved. Only by attracting the best people will you accomplish great deeds."*
>
> **Colin Powell**

SEE IF ANY OF THIS SOUNDS FAMILIAR. When you started your business, adding another employee was a huge step. Actually, if you are like me, you probably weren't starting a *business;* instead, you were creating work for yourself. But you added another carpenter who could free you up a bit so you could sell jobs and do the bookkeeping (such as it was) and order the materials, etc. Now, 8 years later, you have a true business with many employees. That first carpenter rose to be a production assistant to you and now is production manager. Why it's the American Dream, isn't it?

Along the way, you made your high school grad daughter-in-law your bookkeeper and brought your son in to sell. Each time you needed a new employee you reached out to someone who was related, or familiar, or whom you could promote or move from another job in the company. Sounds warm and cozy doesn't it?

Let me shake you out of that warm and cozy American Dream stuff. Here's the reality. You probably have ended up with a hodge podge of folks who aren't superstars in their jobs. You probably have roles that are crazy quilts of tasks stitched together to try and match the skills of the people in them rather than well-thought-out, organized roles with related skills. Because you've homegrown so many on your staff, you've missed out on the valuable knowledge that an experienced job applicant can bring to your company. People may talk about how your company is such a family but they may really be referring to a *dysfunctional* family.

You've been playing neighborhood pickup ball where you choose your team from the folks who happen to be present when you need to fill a role. But your company is now being marginalized by that insular practice. It's time to play pro ball where the roles are carefully designed and described and you search for just the right team players to fill them with a heavy emphasis on aptitude and attitude.

Play Pro Ball

If you're tired of constantly pinch-hitting for weak players, here's how to begin the massive overhaul. I liken it to playing chess. If you are good, you will have the next five moves planned but you'll take them logically and in turn and slowly get where you want to go.

Step One: Draw an organizational chart for the company you want to be. Do some research on how similar remodelers are organized— those who are close in volume and average job size. Read articles, check books, and call up buddies who work in other areas. Then draw up your chart. Make it job centered, not people centered.

Make it departmentalized—for remodelers that usually means administration, marketing, sales, design, and production. Make it hierarchical, showing who reports to whom. Only department heads should report directly to the company owner. If you have a production manager, the carpenters report to that person and that person reports to you. If you have a clerical assistant, that person reports to the office manager and the office manager reports to you.

Step Two: Now draw a chart of your current organization, putting notes beside each box on the major functions each person performs. Rate each person in their job on an alphabetical scale—A, B, or C. Use pluses and minuses. Decide if your company really has room for C players. (The answer is "No!")

Step Three: Figure out how you'll get from where you are now to where you want to be. What steps will it take? Which personnel are keepers and which are not? You'll take only one step at a time because you have to keep the company operating while you do this. And you want to keep the morale as high as possible. Start re-writing job descriptions (yes, writing) for each position.

Step Four: Root out the bad apples. In your employee assessment, did you puzzle over any employee who delivers results well but has serious attitude problems? Maybe they don't adhere to company policy and don't think it really applies to them. Maybe they are highly disrespectful of their co-workers or they talk down about the company, or they walk around with a gray cloud of doom over their head. You have discovered a toxic employee in your midst. They will have to go elsewhere. Try as you might, it is virtually impossible to change attitude and that employee is extremely destructive to the company.

Step Five: Make your first move and let the dust settle. Then make your second move.... But what about the employee with the great attitude who just can't seem to do the job? You have two choices: either train where you think that might work or gently, diplomatically, and empathetically move them on. As you talk with them, let them know you are reorganizing positions and the fit is not there. Give them severance. Let them phase out. You will have pain over doing this, but you are creating a company that will run so much more efficiently, productively, and harmoniously. It will be a company that celebrates excellence and performance and a company that has a healthy—not a dysfunctional—family atmosphere.

Home Schooling

Twenty years ago, when I was traveling the country giving seminars for remodelers, I would suggest that every company needed at least a small budget for staff education. At least one hand would go up. I knew I was going to hear "but if you educate your employees, they will just take that knowledge when they leave and use it to compete against you." Happily, I have not heard that refrain for years.

Today's successful remodeler knows that increasing the knowledge base in his or her company is critical. Indeed it is often one of perhaps 10 factors listed by business experts who differentiate the professionally managed company from the small entrepreneurial company which doesn't provide educational opportunities. The other side of that coin is that today's worker wants to be advancing in their careers and that means advancing in their knowledge.

Hopefully you are taking advantage of the educational opportunities that exist in our business today, which have grown exponentially over the last few years. These include conferences, books and CDs, magazines, peer review groups like our Remodelers Advantage Roundtables, association membership, certifications, and online and live seminars. And, hopefully, you have a budget to educate not only yourself but also your staff.

In your quest for resources, don't overlook using innovative homegrown solutions as well. Here are some you may have missed:

Visits to other remodeling companies.

Our peer group network—Remodelers Advantage Roundtables—encourages and facilitates this highly effective learning activity. But there is nothing to stop you from calling a non-competitive company and suggesting exchange visits. Typically, remodelers are pleased to do this. Everyone wins. Tom Mitchell, president of Mitchell Construction Inc., in Medfield, Mass., is just arranging his fourth visit to another remodeler's operation.

"You want to do some upfront preparation to make the most of the visit," he advises. After a recent visit to the Fisher Group in Annandale, Va., with four of his staff, they revamped their design/build process and design contract within 1 week. "The results of our visit were awesome" says Mitchell. "You get everyone's mind working together. The staff has ownership and they know they are valued. Then they are even pushing me to move ahead with changes."

Creating a custom curriculum to fill a particular need.

When Patty Oehmke of SEI Design Inc., in Vienna, Va., learned that her fellow Roundtables members George and Darlene Gayler, owners of Gayler Construction in Danville, Calif., were trying to fast-track the education of their son, Chris, in the remodeling business, she went into action. She developed a 10-day trip to the East Coast for Gayler with extended visits to four companies. The companies designed a carefully planned curriculum that ran from analyzing financials to shadowing a salesperson on a sales call. Chris Gayler is enthusiastic about his gains. "One of the biggest benefits was seeing how other companies are run first hand, since I've only known the Gayler Construction way," he says. "Each company had their own things they did really well. I'm a visual type of person and it was so helpful to be there."

Holding an annual retreat/planning session.

Fred McDavid, president of Derrick Design & Remodeling Inc., in Huntsville, Ala., holds an all-day lock-the-doors, turn-on-the-answering-machine retreat for all employees at the beginning of each year. The goal is teambuilding. "We want everyone to know their opinions count and how every department's work affects every other," says McDavid. They review the company's strategies, values, and mission and set goals for the year.

Creating a buddy system where senior staff mentors new hires.

Derrick Design & Remodeling has established its own unique orientation for new project manager (lead carpenter) hires, who are paired with a senior project manager. Once the new hire has completed three successful projects as judged on five criteria, they are ready to launch as full-fledged PMs running their own jobs.

Forming a local interest group.

Jeff Rainey, president of Home Equity Builders in Great Falls, Va., began a group to share his knowledge with others. He founded the Remodelers Information Technology Group, which now comprises 20 remodelers who meet for breakfast and listen to a discussion or speaker once a month. "Our concern is to help remodelers who aren't up on the benefits of technology," Rainey says.

So why not analyze your company's educational programming right now? See if you can take it to the next level and start reaping the benefits.

Getting the Right Fit

Want some help in filling your company with happy, intelligent, moral, and supportive employees? I can't imagine you are saying "no." Here are three tools to get you there.

1. First and foremost you need to be happy, intelligent, moral, and supportive. That way, you can model the desired behavior!

2. Next, consider creating a baseline of the personality characteristics that you want in every employee you have. Debra Moore of Custom Design/Build Inc., in Ann Arbor, Mich., has done just that and came up with these desired qualities no matter what position she's hiring for:
   - ➤ high-energy, fast-paced, enthusiastic
   - ➤ client- and service-focused
   - ➤ creative, contributing, flexible
   - ➤ able to work independently
   - ➤ results-driven problem solver
   - ➤ excellent communication skills, including reading and writing
   - ➤ excellent computer/electronics skills
   - ➤ superb follow-through

Now, as Moore recruits and hires (and evaluates current staff), she has a valuable list of behavioral characteristics that will help shape the company culture and working environment.

3. Define the five top core values of your company in writing. While there are hundreds of admirable values like honesty, integrity, teamwork, respect, etc., focus on those you feel are key to your company's successful operation. Get your staff to help you but be sure that you, the owner, have the last word and are satisfied with the result. Values in an entrepreneurial company stream from those of the owner. Define each value and add a couple of behaviors under each that you want to encourage. Then insert these core values into every part of the company—talk about them, use them, reward them, and live them.

Patty McDaniels, owner of Boardwalk Builders Inc., in Rehoboth Beach, Del., did just that with the help of her staff and they came up with these five values that govern how the company does business both internally and externally:

➤ integrity and quality
➤ education
➤ safety
➤ respect and teamwork
➤ profitability

They defined each value and listed desired behaviors. For instance, profitability behaviors are to "Plan effectively and conserve resources to ensure the long-term viability and growth of the company. Complete the job on time and on budget by having the right tools, materials, information, trade contractors, and education."

By modeling the desired behaviors and having defined desired personality characteristics and shared values, you are better prepared to hire effectively and explain the company working environment to prospective hires. You are able to reward appropriate behaviors and discipline those that are non-conforming. And you are able to do it by referring to an agreed-upon standard rather than an arbitrary personal decision.

You will also help everyone in the company move toward a more perfect realization of those values. For instance, you may define "respect for the individual" as one of your company's core values. An individual whose behavior is disrespectful can now be reminded that they are out of line with that agreed-upon guide. An employee who feels that a client has been mistreated can bring that forth with greater assurance. Having written and lived core values means we know how we want to play the game in this company. They call out to us to stretch to perfect our behavior. And that is never bad.

Banish Dysfunction

Two years ago I checked in with the local community foundation to see if they needed volunteers. "Absolutely," said Amy Owen, the executive director. Before I knew it, I was part of one of the very best teams I have ever worked with—a committee with the task of developing three new awards, seeing that they were awarded to worthy recipients, and celebrating those recipients at a gala dinner. The entire committee has just agreed to stay together for the third year and take on a new task.

Why would all these busy volunteers stay together? The work is inspiring but heavy duty. Frankly, it isn't the work we do that's all that great. What *is* really inspiring is the wonderful mix of people who produce—who do more than they say they are going to do, and who really deliver results and deliver them on time. It's an atmosphere where all feel valued, all opinions are worthy, and where the diversity of talent is abundant.

We are all part of teams—our own companies are prime examples. But so is the PTA, the church, the volunteer fire department, and our families. What makes one team work and another flounder? Reading Patrick Lencioni's *Five Dysfunctions of a Team* gave me important insight that has been extremely helpful in working with the company teams that I assess in my role as consultant.

This is another fable-type book—the story of a dysfunctional team that a new CEO is trying to turn around. It is easy reading. Although the title takes a negative slant with the term "dysfunctions" (but what can you expect from someone who also wrote *Death by Meeting*), Lencioni gives a wonderful five-step model for developing an effective team. Each succeeding step depends on the one before it.

It all starts with building *trust* among team members. Trusting team members admit mistakes and weaknesses, ask for help, take risks in offering feedback and assistance, and offer and accept apologies without hesitation. Lencioni offers some practical ways to build trust, which include the leader modeling and rewarding these behaviors, personality profiling (and sharing those profiles), or just simply learning more about each other personally.

"Trust is the confidence among team members that their peers' intentions are good, and that there is no reason to be protective or careful around the group," notes Lencioni.

And trust allows the team to engage in *healthy conflict*—the second quality of a great team. Thus, they have lively meetings, hear ideas from every member, solve problems quickly, and put critical topics on the table for discussion.

Now the table is set for the team members to have *commitment*—clarity and buy-in—to whatever is decided. "As simple as it seems, " writes Lencioni, "one of the tools for ensuring commitment is the use of clear deadlines for when decisions will be made and honoring those dates with discipline and rigidity."

Have you ever wished you had greater *accountability* among your staff? Accountability is the willingness of team members to call their peers on performance or behaviors that might hurt the team. As Lencioni notes, "there is nothing like the fear of letting down respected teammates that motivates people to improve their performance." This places primary responsibility for accountability on the team, not the owner. For most company owners, that would be a joy!

Could there be anything else? Yes, there is step five. And that is a focus on the *results*. The outcome from your team's laser-like focus is that you will retain achievement-oriented staff, you will get goals accomplished, and all will learn from any failures and bask in the delight of the successes.

Lencioni also has a workbook of exercises that you can use to put his principles in action. You could have your key managers read one chapter a month of his *Five Dysfunctions* book and spend time in their meeting discussing it and how it applies to their work. You could have every employee take the assessment in the back and see where your team might be weak. This team-building model is a great resource. It's not a quick fix but any steps your team can take in the right direction should pay off many times over.

Trust, healthy conflict, commitment, accountability, and results—now I know why I like my committee-team and why I signed up to work hard for no money for another year.

Misery or Ministry?

Author Patrick Lencioni provides everything a good business book needs. His titles are compelling—*Death by Meeting, The Three Signs of a Miserable Job, The Five Temptations of a CEO*. He is a very good writer of both fiction and non-fiction and that is key because his books first tell a fable dramatizing his points and then he has a final section teaching his system more directly. Most importantly, Lencioni bites off just the right size topic and right number of key points so that his books are digestible, substantive, and memorable. And he does all this in a short, easy-to-read book devoid of jargon.

In *The Three Signs of a Miserable Job*, Lencioni writes of Brian Bailey, a successful executive newly and unexpectedly retired when his company is sold. He has money but he doesn't have work. Full retirement in a vacation community doesn't agree with him and he soon is part owner and part manager of a down-at-the-heels pizza restaurant.

He is challenged by trying out his management ideas on a lackluster staff in going-nowhere jobs. When his relatively unorthodox approach to turning this small company around works, he takes on a temporary assignment at a mid-sized company, where his turnaround by combating these three enemies of enthusiasm and fulfillment is once again successful.

So what are those three signs of a miserable job and even more importantly, how do you overcome and eliminate them? The first is *anonymity*. "People who see themselves as invisible, generic, or anonymous cannot love their jobs, no matter what they are doing," Lencioni maintains.

To banish anonymity, managers—especially direct supervisors—need to take a personal interest in the employee, her goals, his interests outside work, and his family. It's simple but it takes some one-on-one time. "People want to be managed as people, not as mere workers," advises Lencioni.

The second is *irrelevance*. If we cannot make the connection between our work and the satisfaction of others, we won't find a reason to continuously improve and we won't find fulfillment in our work. Each of us needs to know that our work matters and that our job has a bigger significance.

For frontline people like carpenters, the connection is obvious but our behind-the-scenes staff may not see a direct connection. Their beneficiaries may be you as owner or may be other staff members. To establish relevance means answering two questions—who am I helping in my job and how am I helping them? This needs to be an ongoing dialogue between manager and worker. Getting input from the team on how this individual's performance affects their ability to do their job well is also key.

The third sign is a word Lencioni invented—*immeasurement*. Each of us needs to be able to measure our progress in getting better at our job and knowing when we have been successful. Frankly, we hear in every business book that improvement for both the individual and the company is about metrics, metrics, and metrics.

Lencioni emphasizes that the individual needs to do the measurement and sometimes it is subjective. In Lencioni's fable, Carl, who mans the pizza drive-by window, had two metrics to measure—the number of smiles he received (happy customer) and the number of orders delivered without missing items. When an item was missed by Carl, it made for a less-than-happy client and it threw the kitchen into emergency mode.

I still remember once being mesmerized by a female traffic controller at a road construction site who was definitely high impact in her super anonymous job. It's been 15 years and I can still see her dancing her signals with genuine joy, waving and smiling as she did a great job. She made me smile as I waited. I learned that day that any job can be made special to those who work with you and are dependent on you.

One of Brian's major "aha's" is to see management as a ministry. Helping workers be enthusiastic about their work and pass that enthusiasm on to their customers, family, and co-workers is important work. Lencioni writes, "…the real shame is not that more people aren't working in positions of service to others, but that so many managers haven't yet realized that they already are." Are you thinking of your people management duties as a miserable job or as a ministry where you can perform exceptional service for so many people and their families? If it's the former, grab this book and devour it.

Bedrock and Boundaries

I've just come from a meeting of 15 very different people who have long-term business relationships with each other and with my company. Important issues surfaced: what is our goal as a group, how do we fit into a system of many groups, how do we want to govern ourselves, and what will be the underlying rules that create an infrastructure that supports the success of the group?

I don't have to tell you that if you have 15 people working on anything (think—your company), they will be very different in how they view the challenge and what solution seems just right to each participant. They may even disagree on how to go about disagreeing.

Some will feel they know the right way to do everything, won't understand why others don't fully agree, and will be relatively quick to anger when things don't go their way. Others will want to research the issue into oblivion, get totally bogged down in the details, and be largely driven by the fear of being wrong. There will be some who consider the issue logically, want to work as a team, and are patient and listen well but want to follow a leader.

And there undoubtedly will be some who love working and influencing others, may talk too much, want a collegial decision, and are overly optimistic that everything will just "work out." And, of course, there will be lots of folks in our group or company who represent a mix of all these traits in unique combinations. How do we get anything done in groups?

There is another key player here—your company within which these folks are operating. There are undoubtedly rules, procedures, and systems that impact just how much leeway there is for change. Oh, I forgot another hugely important player for you—the client, who has their own unique personality, style, needs, wants, and expectations. And maybe even an architect and/or interior designer.

In a successful company, "the company way" creates the platform for everyone's success in their job, success in delivery to the client, and success for the company's continued operation. But that "way" must allow leeway for change, input, and empowerment. In most challenges, there is no major conflict. In some of the most difficult challenges, the company owner walks a fine line and must make some Solomon-like calls after listening to divergent opinions.

For me, this is where zooming back out to the big picture is so helpful. I call up the company mission, the values, the key systems that have enabled our clients to be successful, and our process to be supportive and cutting edge and the company to be successful. For me it is going back to bedrock, to the boundaries that must not be crossed and then seeing how much leeway there is for change, new ideas, and innovation.

It may sound simple on paper, but it is not. How do you make these "there may be no clearly right answer" calls? How do you accommodate all the personalities in your organization? (And, by the way, if you don't have a rainbow of personality styles in your organization, you need that diversity of viewpoints.) What is bedrock in your organization? Where are your boundaries which cannot be crossed? What are the values that can't be tarnished? Be sure you have this well thought through before you meet a critical challenge.

The business books tell you to listen, listen, and listen to your staff. Get everything out on the table without rancor. The books also tell you that listening and acknowledging, and then doing what can be done and explaining what can't be changed keeps almost all those unique players happy.

While I was in the midst of my challenges with these 15 caring clients who have the best of intentions, who just want to improve the system, who want to pioneer a new path, I was next to a remodeler who used every break to work and try to figure out whether to take a $1 million job with a client who wanted to bend his rules and was angry and demanding. I could almost hear the conflict grinding through his mind as he weighed the alternatives. The right path is not clear; there are competing interests and we must make some leaps of faith based on our bedrock.

Increasing Hiring Wins

I bet you are spending more and more time in the hiring mode—especially if you are growing your company. Perhaps you are that rare remodeler who looks at hiring as a tremendous opportunity. Most of us sigh and dread going back out into the marketplace to recruit, sift, interview, and hire. Typically, we are stretched for time—that's why we're hiring. Then comes the training period (hopefully), when time is short and yet we have to invest even more time in the new employee. And we may have chosen the wrong person and have to live through the nightmare of letting them go and rehiring.

Let's rethink our approach.

Each time we hire we have an opportunity to add a new superstar to our team. This should be a time of rejoicing and renewed zeal to define the job, define the attitude and values we want, and find the very best fit. Here is some data to back up the value of putting that extra energy into your search for the right candidate.

An analysis done of 80 productivity studies by Hunter, Schmidt, and Judasch (reported in the *Journal of Applied Psychology*, 1990, vol. 75, no.1) showed the productivity gains which could be attained by hiring the top 1% of workers in any category over the bottom 1%. In a low-complexity job like fast-food worker, the top 1% were three times more productive. In a medium-complexity job like accountant or factory team leader, the top 1% were 12 times more effective, and in a high-complexity job like executive or salesperson, the differential was "infinite."

Let's assume you don't hire that bottom 1%. The study also looked at the productivity of the top 1% versus the mean average in each of the three complexity categories. A top worker in a low-complexity job will be 52% more productive than the average worker. In a medium-complexity job, the top employee will beat the average by 85%, and in a highly complex job, the difference is 127%.

Does it pay to hold out for the very best? It certainly seems to. But how will we know them when we see them? We need a hiring system. We can build it as we go and add to it with each hire. Eventually, we'll have everything in place to make our hiring as effective and efficient as possible. Here are some of the component parts you want to put in place:

➤ A recruitment plan that works to bring you enough qualified candidates. This takes experimenting. Begin to build a stable of ads, fliers, and referral programs that work for your company. Hiring has become a marketing activity for companies. To get the best, you need to talk benefits and have a user-friendly system.

➤ Develop a quick and friendly screening system that weeds out the unqualified. This will vary for different positions. Make this portion quick and easy for the candidates and for your company.

➤ Decide how you will interview. One West Coast company, starved for carpenters and helpers, is experimenting with 15-minute initial field interviews with their current carpenters. Only after a candidate passes muster will they then be interviewed by the production manager. Good candidates get jobs fast, so be sure your system isn't too cumbersome.

➤ Have up-to-date job descriptions to distribute. They make a great interview tool to discuss how your position relates to their skills and past experience. Hiring experts emphasize exploring how the candidate's values and attitude fit the company culture. These can be explored through carefully composed interview questions.

➤ Get outside help where possible. For instance, your accountant could interview your bookkeeper candidate.

➤ Use personality profiles to match the final one or two candidates' innate behaviors with those needed for the job. Don't hire if the match is not there. This step alone will improve your hiring by 30 to 50%.

➤ Be sure to run a drug test and a driving and criminal record check before hiring. Be clear upfront that those items will be required.

➤ And, of course, check those referrals in as creative a way as you can. Would the former employer rehire?

A good hiring system is a journey, not a destination. Start where you are and work toward what you want to have. Add one piece at a time and soon you'll have a system for hiring those top 10%—or 5%—or 1% of highly productive folks.

The Power of Group Thinking

Have you ever played one of those educational survivor games? They typically have you shipwrecked or plane wrecked with a group of individuals and what appears to be a random collection of salvageable items. You have to rank the usefulness of those items in helping the group survive. You do your own ranking first and then you work in a small group to rank the items after listening to all opinions. Then there is a whole lot of scoring and comparing.

What you learn beyond a doubt is not only some survival tips but also that group-think surpasses individual brainpower almost every time. About 80 to 90% of groups get a score higher than that of any individual in their group. If you weren't already realizing just how powerful group thinking is, these games are a fun way to settle the issue.

So why don't we owners share more of our company challenges with our staff? Why don't we get everyone working on how we will achieve a 40% gross profit? Or how we'll sell and produce $750,000 this year? Or how we can streamline the sales-to-production handoff? Or how we might create an incentive for our staff?

For some remodelers, this openness just comes naturally. But for most, it is very scary. For years they've been the "Little Red Hen" doing everything for the company. Often, their first hires are poor ones while they learn how to be a more accomplished hirer. They hide their financial reports, being sure that their 3% net will cause a revolt among their employees.

Even more prevalent is the idea that when a system, or a checklist, or a list of core values is needed, that the simplest, quickest, and most efficient way to get it done is for the owner to do it for everyone. And that is the simplest, quickest, and most efficient way to get it done.

But then how do we sell to our staff what we have developed? That is the hard part. They don't "own" it. There is no buy-in. In fact, there may well be resistance and argument. Yes, we saved time on the front end but we're losing it in implementation and, in fact, we may fail overall.

So if we look at the entire process of devising a solution, applying it, improving it, and making it a habit, then the simplest, quickest, and most efficient way is by involving everyone from the start. Not only that, but the group is likely to come up with a better solution! Group-think is not neat and tidy. Democracy takes longer, but the results are much better.

You learn some other important concepts from these survival games. You learn about consensus. How does a group of varying opinion get to a final decision after they have heard all the different ideas? It's sort of like a jury. There is usually a prevailing decision and those who are less enthusiastic about it need to agree they can live with it. So these games teach the meaning of consensus in decision-making.

On those few occasions when an individual in a group scores higher than the group itself, it usually signals that whoever was the group leader did not get everyone's input. We all recognize there are more-vocal and less-vocal folks. The best solution might lie with the latter, so the group leader needs to be able to pull out the best from everyone.

These games also teach the importance of developing the right strategy before you start answering what you think is the question. Depending on whether the group decides its best survival strategy is sending the two hardiest members for help, or that all will stay together and wait to be discovered or all members will hike to help, the rankings of the salvage items change drastically. If half the members are thinking one solution and the others are figuring another, we know we'll have dissension because we haven't decided our basic strategy yet.

I haven't even mentioned one of the biggest benefits of fully utilizing the brainpower of everyone in your company. It frees you up as owner. You are preparing your company for your 4-week trip to Fiji. By the time you leave, you know they'll be equipped to handle the toughest problems together. So start planning which bathing suit you are going to pack. Share the good, the bad, and the ugly with your staff and stand back and prepare to be surprised by just how well they do.

Freeing Up a Future

Oh, that Donald Trump. He's made "You're fired!" a household phrase. Maybe some of that will trickle down to business. You can't be in business very long without needing to fire someone. Unfortunately, none of us mortals do it with such vigor and enthusiasm.

Most of us are sloppy hirers and terrible, procrastinating firers. Needless to say, these two traits spell chaos in a small company where every position is a key position. If we can't be enthusiastic firers, maybe we can at least be competent. What are some of the issues that hold us back?

➤ We know too much about the hardships of the employee's life and realize this may be one more blow to their self-esteem and financial security.

➤ We hate to hire and so we watch for that occasional tiny glimmer that they may truly have the motivation or the skills or the attitude to handle the job effectively.

➤ We blame ourselves for not spending enough time coaching them. Maybe we haven't really given them a chance.

➤ We hate or fear confrontation. What if they blow up during the meeting? What if they demand detailed justification for our action?

➤ The employee in question is related to us or related to another valued employee, making for a very sticky situation.

So let's assume we know what we need to do. We need to free up their future (and ours) by acknowledging they do not fit the position and the company's needs. It is time to fire, terminate, and dismiss. Here are some tips:

➤ Prepare carefully for your meeting. Consult your attorney to be sure all your legal ducks are in a row. Hopefully you have been writing up infractions and counseling sessions and putting them in the employee's file.

➤ Script what you plan to say and say only that. Give the true reasons for the dismissal but state it in terms of the business' needs. Within reason, let the employee save face. But don't get drawn into revisiting your decision or arguing your case. You may be angry, but stay very businesslike in this meeting. Speak slowly and softly. If there are tears, stay quiet until they subside.

➤ Ask the person to return their key, company credit cards, gas cards, and any communication equipment or company possessions immediately. Assess whether you should change door locks and computer passwords and take any other security steps.

➤ Experts advise asking the employee to leave the premises immediately. You will want to have boxes on hand so they can remove their possessions.

A friend who recently was advised to fire someone felt he could not live with this advice and gave the employee the choice to remain under certain rules for up to 2 weeks. Ultimately the fired employee left after a week, finding the situation too difficult. This is definitely a gray area.

The point is that firing someone is a nasty task, and nobody (but the Donald) likes it. However, the health of your company rests on the quality of your team. Having to go through this difficult situation may even convince you that prevention—by more careful hiring—may be just the road you need to take. And that would be (as Martha Stewart says) "a good thing."

Membership in Your Company

Have you ever thought of employment by your company as membership? Using this membership concept helps to emphasize the key benefits today's hires want—a great working environment and strong relationships that build a sense of community within the business.

As a company owner who wants to attract top-quality staff to become members and stay members, you'll certainly have to design a market rate package of tangible benefits (pay, benefits, title, perks). But the success of your hiring and retention will ultimately rely on your intangible benefits.

You are sure to bring in lots of fun and laughs and good humor. You're careful to keep competition alive between employees but not foremost. You stress teamwork. You model the behavior you want to see in your community and you reward that behavior at every turn. Rewards can range from the fun and simple to the fancy and more expensive.

At Derrick Design & Remodeling, Inc., in Huntsville, Ala., employees wanted to improve meetings. "It always seemed like in meetings all we heard about was what we did wrong, how we should have, could have, done." says Sharon Bufkin, design development consultant. "But we never heard 'hey, great job' on the things we did right or where we went the extra mile to get it done right."

The company printed up wooden nickels with its logo. "We pass one on to fellow employees for a job well done or when they go out of their way to make things better on a job," says Bufkin. "We now have included our clients. When they sign a development agreement, we offer them the opportunity to participate. We keep a record of the nickels for each employee. Then they receive a certificate from a rewards program we found online (www.awardsnetwork.com). They are points put toward the 'purchase' of an item of their choice, depending on the points they have acquired. We have had a good time with the new system. It helps all of us to look toward the positive."

At Marrokal Construction Company in Lakeside, Calif., business manager Lori Bryan reports that employee recognition has many facets, including the following:

➤ Referral letters from clients are read in front of the entire team at the weekly staff meeting. The superintendent is given a $100 gift certificate personalized for something that he would enjoy. The letter is also sent to all trade contractors who worked on the job.

➤ An "Employee of the Quarter" and "Trade Contractor of the Quarter" is voted on by all employees. Winners are recognized in front of the entire team during a Friday meeting and are given a commemorative award and a gift with a value of approximately $250 that is selected personally for the recipient. The event is captured in the company newsletter, which is sent to clients and all current trade contractors.

➤ At the Christmas party, each employee receives a vacation trip for two (to Hawaii, Mexico, etc.) valued at about $2,000. The benefit is two-fold: Employees get to take vacations they may not normally take, and Marrokal gets a well-rested employee.

➤ If the company's goals are attained at the end of the year, each department holds a celebration of its own. This year included the production team going to Vegas for the weekend (including airfare, lodging, and a show), the design team going to Cabo San Lucas for a weekend, and the admin team going to an off-Broadway show and dinner.

➤ Every year rodeo tickets are offered to all employees, trade contractors and their employees, and families. This year Marrokal purchased over 500 rodeo tickets! A catered barbecue for everyone on the afternoon of the rodeo is included.

➤ Employees and their spouse/guest are taken to the Del Mar Thoroughbred track. The event is first class, with seating in the sky-box area, a great lunch, and $100 per person provided for betting.

Rob Matthews and Robin Burrill of Curb Appeal Renovations in Ft. Worth, Texas, search for unique opportunities to give spur-of-the-moment thank-you's throughout the year. Their expressions of appreciation have included personal vehicle repairs, home repairs, and help during a new-home purchase. "The only way we know how or when to do these things is because we talk to our employees," says Burrill. "I don't know if it is necessarily the gift that means the most as it is the fact that we're paying attention to what is going on in their lives and help them out when they need it the most."

So how are you doing in attracting and keeping employee membership? While expressing appreciation is only one piece of many, it is a key factor in developing a positive work environment. Wherever possible, include fun, publicize the special moment to the entire company and to the employee's family, and customize the reward.

Accentuate the Positive

I apologized for something I did. Word of my apology traveled the grapevine. Soon, a small card arrived in the mail from Craig Durosko at Sun Design Remodeling Specialists in Burke, Va. The front of the card says, "Hero of the Day!" Open it up and there's a personal note from Craig thanking me for making amends. All around the card are written types of actions that could lead to your getting just such a special note—teamwork, conflict resolution, charity, truth, and fun.

This card has taken up precious space on my desk for months. I feel good every time it catches my eye. As Mark Twain once said, "I can live for 2 months on a good compliment." A recent Gallup poll discovered that 65% of Americans received no praise or recognition at work last year! It's free, it's easy, and it's powerful. Use legitimate praise lavishly in your business and watch the transformation.

"While money is important to employees, what tends to motivate them to perform—and to perform at higher levels—is the thoughtful, personal kind of recognition that signifies true appreciation for a job well done" writes author Bob Nelson in his nifty little book *1001 Ways to Reward Employees.*

Nelson maintains there are really only three simple guidelines for effectively rewarding and recognizing employees:
1. Match the reward to the person. Make what you do have a very personal, customized fit.

2. Match the reward to the achievement. In other words, take into account the significance of the achievement.

3. Be timely and specific. Reward as soon as possible after the desired behavior or achievement.

Michael Spreckelmeier, owner of Progressive Builders, Inc., in Ft. Myers, Fla., is a letter writer extraordinaire. And he is always on the lookout for something to praise. Here's a quote from just one of his handwritten letters of praise to an employee: "You are doing a wonderful job. Don't take my word for it. You can see the difference in our company.… You have always been talented and able to get the job done. However, now you are talented, a great manager, and a team player who can get many jobs done." That letter is not going in the trash anytime soon.

"It is my belief that money is indeed appreciated by employees, but recognition for a job well done is very important as well," says Spreckelmeier. "I love to praise. It is one of my most favorite activities."

Here are four more great ideas from remodelers:

➤ "I keep $25 gift cards in my office and hand them out a couple of times a month—usually Outback Steak House or gas cards. They let someone know I value their effort," says Bob Benedict of Northwood Construction in Sterling, Va.

➤ "We have two Employee of the Month awards that recognize exceptional service," says Kevin O'Brien of Agape Construction in Kirkwood, Mo. "One is for production and one for administration. They get a framed certificate describing what they did and how that exemplified the core values of the company. It comes with a $50 gift certificate and their name is engraved on a brass plaque in the office."

➤ Janeen Welsh of Welsh Construction, Lexington, Virginia also has an Employee of the Month program with a $20 award given at the full staff meeting. If there is not a good reason to award it one month, then the award dollars build up until someone has done something beyond the call of duty.

➤ Patty McDaniel spreads the ability to reward around. The production manager has a $750 fund to award lunch, doughnuts, gift cards, or cash bonuses as recognition. The office manager has a $1,000 fund to reward timely and accurate paperwork.

I would add another guideline to Bob Nelson's three. The world of remodeling seems to push us into a "punchlist mentality." We look constantly for what is wrong. We've got to be equally vigilant about finding what is right. Seek it out. For most of us, it calls for a change in our behavior. But what a powerful change it is. And what a powerful impact it has on the working environment of our company.

Systematic Disney

There's nothing Mickey Mouse about Disney Enterprises. There is a lot for a remodeler to learn from their systematic approach to wowing the families who visit their world-class theme parks. How do they deliver first-rate service when they pay their employees no more than market rate and when most of those employees are young and relatively inexperienced? It's definitely worth reading about, and you have a full shelf of books to choose from. I started with Be *Our Guest: Perfecting the Art of Customer Service* from the Disney Institute.

When Walt Disney first discussed the development of a theme park with his wife, she was dismayed because "they are so dirty." But, said Walt, that was exactly why he wanted to create with a new brush. Today, Walt Disney World in Orlando is the largest single-site employer in the United States. It is run by a "cast" of 55,000 and is open every day of the year.

Underlying the near-perfect delivery of service is a strong core ideology. It starts with a service theme that has evolved over the years—"We create happiness by providing the finest in entertainment for people of all ages, everywhere." This theme defines the organization's purpose or mission (creating happiness), communicates an internal message about how it will be delivered (through the finest in entertainment), and creates an image of the organization. What is your service theme?

Writers such as Tom Peters (*In Search of Excellence*) and Jim Collins and Jerry Porras (*Built to Last*) have stressed that excellent companies all have powerful service themes well embedded in the organization. But that is not enough to help employees do their daily work and make the myriad decisions needed each day.

Underlying this service theme are four Disney service standards, or service values. In prioritized order, they are Safety, Courtesy, Show, and Efficiency. They are meant to be filters to enable staff to judge and prioritize their actions. What are the service standards that will enable your staff to make appropriate decisions to further the client experience?

But how is quality service delivered in such a way that it wows, entertains, and delivers more than the promises? Disney has isolated these three delivery systems—Cast, Setting, and Process.

In Disney-speak, Cast = employees. Every world-class organization delivers through well-chosen, well-trained, and well-motivated staff. And no one does it better than Disney. How are you doing?

Setting is Disney-speak for the physical area where your guests (clients) meet you. Or, to get more technical, "Setting is the environment in which service is delivered to customers, all of the objects within that environment, and the procedures used to enhance and maintain the service environment and objects." Disney World distinguishes Backstage (no clients) and Onstage (the public areas). Your setting is certainly the jobsite and probably your office. It's the vehicles your folk drive and the tools they use. How are you doing there?

Processes are the policies, tasks, and procedures that are used to deliver service. They are critical. They need to be designed from the client's point of view. If a guest has a complaint, it is a "combustion point" and must be handled before it becomes an "explosion."

Great effort is expended at Disney World to anticipate common combustion points and work at preventing them. Standing in long lines was a frequently heard complaint and there is an entire program designed to reduce upset, allow for visit planning, and create honest expectations around just this issue. What are your clients' common combustion points? What standard ways do you have to prevent them and to handle them when they arise?

I hope this essay sends you scurrying out for a book on the Disney systems. I checked Amazon.com, which listed 82 and there were 4 different free lists of favorite Disney business books. There is so much that is fun to read about (did you know Walt Disney started making short films at 18 in his family's garage?) and so much that could be adapted creatively to the hairy remodeling process. I am challenging you to get out of your comfort zone and add a little Mickey Mouse to your company.

Vitamin P

I wonder how my new puppy would improve if I corrected and praised her only every 6 months. How well would your children learn under the same circumstances? The answer is obvious—they simply wouldn't learn to conform to our needs and rules. And how do your employees do with that every-6-months-whether-you-need-it-or-not review?

Supervisors and the supervised frequently dread performance reviews. And if they are linked to potential pay raises, the staffer listens to every comment with an eye to whether it might, or might not, mean a raise. "You are a good multi-tasker," says the supervisor. "A raise," thinks the employee. "But you tend to drop the ball where putting things in writing is concerned," continues the supervisor. "Uh-oh, maybe no raise," thinks the employee.

A recent article on reviews in *The Washington Post* began, "Oh, those employee reviews. They make the worker bees feel as if they're walking into the principal's office. And the managers find them even worse...." But if your job includes training, mentoring, and coaching, how do you improve on this age old process?

Here are some tips.

> Train all supervisors to give *constant feedback* to those they supervise. That feedback should be primarily positive and sincere and only secondarily negative. The negative critiques should focus on practical ways to improve.
>
> One of the best books on this subject (and it is an easy read) is *The One Minute Manager*, by Ken Blanchard. The author writes about giving 1-minute praises and 1-minute critiques. He advises making them concise and to the point. In this way your folks get constant mentoring and coaching. There is no way they will walk into reviews wondering what you or their supervisor thinks of them.

> Do semi-annual reviews but make them enlightening and mostly positive for the staffer. Take them to lunch or breakfast or arrive at the jobsite with coffee and danish for a quiet (but scheduled) chat. Get their summary of how things have been going. As in your sales calls, take time

to develop rapport. Talk about their personal goals and their company goals. Ask what skills they are working on and what they see they might need to improve.

After listening for a half hour, it's your turn to talk about the improvements you've seen. Pat them on the back for the growth they've made. Then discuss how they might move to the next level in their work. End by agreeing on an area they will work to improve and discuss how the company can help. Should they take a course? Should they visit another remodeler? Should they work with another carpenter who will help them?

➤ But, you might say, what if I have a really poor worker or someone with a really poor attitude and there's little to be positive about? The answer is simple—you shouldn't have this person on staff. Everyone on your staff should meet minimal requirements and be a constant improver with goals which you help set.

In all your feedback, be sure you are evaluating, praising, and critiquing not only their job performance skills and their results but also their attitude—their acceptance of the company's core values.

➤ Divorce pay from reviews. In the best of all worlds you will have adopted a pay-for-skill policy which makes clear what you have to do to achieve a certain level of pay. But even if you haven't (and 99.9% of remodelers haven't), make pay announcements apart from reviews. Keep the focus of the review on the acknowledgement of improvements and the setting of new goals.

➤ Consider asking your employees for advice and help in devising a performance review program. By getting them involved and getting consensus upfront, you'll have much more buy-in with the program you develop.

➤ Go wild. At the end of each review, ask the employee to answer these questions as quickly and honestly as they can:
  - What would you like me to stop doing?
  - What would you like me to continue doing?
  - What would you like to start doing that I am not doing now?

Performance reviews are an important and effective part (but only a part) of an ongoing mentoring and coaching program. Do them but don't forget the day-to-day honest feedback, which is even more important.

Spreading Good Cheer

Gary Stokes of ADR Builders, Ltd., a remodeling company in Timonium, Md., is a great gift giver. At a recent dinner for his company and a number of peer remodelers, he gave out unexpected and very personalized awards suited to each of the 20 recipients. Each award was accompanied by a unique and personal gift. It was a wow. I went over to his wife and partner, Jane Stokes, and said, "What a wonderful job you guys did in finding just the right gift for each person." "Oh, no," she said, "Gary did it all." His thoughtfulness elevated simple generosity to a very special moment.

December is month of religious holidays and special occasions. It's the time when you express your love and caring for so many—often with a gift. Why not do what Gary did and make that gift very personal? If you have five employees, it shouldn't be hard. Maybe you own a relatively big company—say 40 employees. Then, you might buy special gifts for your key managers and have them decide on and purchase uniquely fitting gifts for each of their staff.

Now I want to raise the ante. How about those special subcontractors who help your company shine? Are there suppliers who go the extra mile for you? Include them in your gift giving.

Let's raise the ante again. Each gift could be accompanied by a handwritten, sincere, and positive note. If you have those 40 employees, it might take you 4 hours to do the notes. Not much time in the big picture to let each of your staff know you care about them. Just a thought.

Over the year, you could give many gifts to your staff. Here are just a few:

➤ Fire that toxic employee who may get results in their job but does it by stomping on your culture, disregarding your procedures, and riling others.

➤ Take each employee to lunch by themselves with the express purpose of learning more about them personally.

➤ Create a safe psychological environment where each worker feels welcome to suggest solutions and to work toward streamlining how things are done in your company.

➤ Make your company an "intentional learning community" where learning how to be a better person and a better worker is encouraged, funded, and rewarded.

➤ Give your staff ideals, visions, missions to believe in. We spend one-third of our time at work and want it to count for something bigger than we are.

➤ Abolish overtime except in an unusual crisis. This goes for office workers as well. One-third of your life is enough to spend at work.

Someone sent me (and many others) one of those e-mail attachments. I don't usually read them, but this one I opened. I'll share part of it here:

"If we could shrink the earth's population to a village of precisely 100 people, with all the existing human ratios remaining the same, it would look something like the following:

➤ 80 would live in substandard housing

➤ 70 would be unable to read

➤ 50 would suffer from malnutrition

➤ 1 would be near death; 1 would be near birth

➤ 1 would have a college education.

➤ 6 would possess 59% of the entire world's wealth and all 6 would be from the United States."

Guard Those Systems

It was a wonderful dinner party with a fun group of remodeling-related folks. During dinner the hosting couple, who share a remodeling company, started to banter about their differing styles of leadership. She and the office manager were planning to lay down the law to the field on timely and accurate submission of time cards. They were tired of trying to cajole, beg, and nag for that important information. He, in mock despair, pleaded for patience—"We need these guys." Clearly he was concerned that if the company got too stringent on enforcing procedures, some valued field personnel might walk.

In their big-city location, they are paying $20 per hour for helpers and $28 to $35 per hour for lead carpenters. Their benefit package is very generous and bonuses are plentiful. Yet this company is still having trouble finding as many field personnel as they need to produce their fine-quality work. No question; this could be seen as a dilemma.

I was a dinner guest that night, so I resisted the temptation to put on my consultant's hat. While the topic seemed pretty trivial, it had deep roots in two areas that are crucial to running a successful business. So now let me tell you what the consultant inside was thinking.

The web of systems that a company develops may well be the most valuable part of the business. In fact, when you purchase a franchise, you are buying systems they advertise as leading to success. What does one entrepreneur bring to the table that is different from any other remodeler?

It's their hard-won success system that they've learned from experience. They've developed a way to do business that helps make success predictable. You simply can't let an employee—even a very valued one—take this from you. The whole world conspires to destroy your systems. But in the end, what do you really have other than your unique way of doing business?

Ultimately, to be successful in remodeling you have to develop a strong group of systems and procedures and you have to enforce discipline in yourself and your staff to follow them. If everyone who worked at McDonald's was allowed to cook the french fries their way, McDonald's wouldn't be the global success story that it is. You can't let anyone destroy your unique approach to accomplishing remodeling. If time cards are the way you do business, there is no negotiation. If someone has a better idea, they can suggest it and lobby for it until it is the accepted system.

A second issue is in play when you feel an employee is so valuable that you begin to change the rules for them—when you don't feel you can ask them to adhere to a system. You are being held hostage and you simply can't afford to be. In the dinner table situation above, this issue was relatively mild with lots of joking.

However, I often work with remodelers who are in tortuous situations with a high-performing individual who won't follow the rules. In truth, all the employees in the company are watching this drama play out to see if rules are fairly applied. While you may even think you can't survive without this employee or you'll never be able to replace them, I have learned that the outcome of taking action is usually just the opposite.

Many employees move back into line when challenged. And if they don't, you have to take action to "free up their future." Once this toxic employee is let go, everyone breathes a sigh of relief and the toxic employee's replacement is often better.

So guard your systems and procedures and be sure everyone values them and follows them—including the boss!

Brainstorming

Today's news noted that the heads of Afghanistan and Pakistan were going to visit the White House for a "brainstorming session." Hmm. I'm picturing the president with flip chart and markers.

Actually, brainstorming is a fun, creative way to get people awake and contributing. It can be a tremendous tool in the business toolbox. It was invented by advertising executive Alex Osborn in the 1940's when he was looking for a technique that would help groups generate lots of new ideas.

Brainstorming simply means turning a group of employees loose to generate as many ideas as possible in a limited time span (20 to 30 minutes) to solve a problem. For instance, the question might be "How can we get quality leads from the top interior designers in our area?" or "What could we do for our clients to raise their spirits during the most difficult part of their remodeling?" or "How can we get more applicants for our field jobs?"

The question is asked, the timer is started, and someone writes down all the ideas—wacky or sane—on a flip chart. Hopefully, folks will shout out so many ideas that the scribe has difficulty keeping up and someone starts taping sheets of ideas to the walls. Each new idea sparks a flurry of others.

Even such a free-flowing activity is best served by following some guidelines:

- ➤ No criticism is allowed. People must feel safe to say nearly anything.
- ➤ Quantity is king. Don't focus on quality—only quantity—because quantity will ultimately include quality.
- ➤ No discussion of an idea is allowed because that slows the flow.
- ➤ Zany ideas are welcome since they often spark useful ideas.
- ➤ Folks are encouraged to build off each other's ideas.
- ➤ Be sure to set a time limit.

There is a form of brainstorming that can give you a very productive start. It's called a SWOT analysis. The letters stand for strengths, weaknesses, opportunities, and threats. Think of the first two as relating to internal issues and opportunities and threats as being external.

I recently asked a number of remodelers to conduct just such a SWOT exercise with their planning teams. Here are some sample results. Strengths included "being design/build," "name recognition," and "strong vendor relationships." Among the weaknesses listed were "subcontractors not reliable, damaging to client relationships," "time lag in scheduling warranty work," and "lack of shared vision."

"Urban migration," "high home equity," and "use of showroom as a sales tool," were some examples of opportunities. Threats included, "too reliant on company owner," "unsatisfied customers," "terrorism," and "not owning own office building."

You can not only use SWOT analysis at the company level; it can be very useful to employ it at the departmental level in your planning process. You want to enhance your strengths and eliminate your weaknesses. For instance, your SWOT on estimating might turn up these challenges—outdated software, too many estimates being generated for number of jobs being sold, lack of timeliness in estimating, and a 6% erosion in job costs (some of which is likely due to inaccurate estimates). Create a plan to address each one with focused goals and clear metrics or measurements.

Hopefully, you won't have the same towering threat one remodeling wag had: "employee breaks an e-mail chain, bringing curse upon company."

Role Playing

"No, that's being too aggressive!" "No, if anything he's being too soft." Both these statements were said about how the same remodeler demonstrated his sales technique with another remodeler acting as prospect.

I've just finished facilitating two meetings for remodelers where we spent a half day demonstrating and working on how a remodeler might handle a number of situations.

We were role playing. A group member would set up an issue they were having difficulty with. Then they would play the remodeler and another attendee would be the prospect or client.

Role playing is so useful for working through just the right "scripting"— whether it's how you answer the phone, take a lead, ask a prospect to take the next step in sales, or handle an unhappy client. It's a great teaching tool that can be used throughout your company. It takes a while to get used to having the spotlight on you while you go through your paces, but the tone of the observers should be one of helpfulness and support.

What did I learn from these demonstrations?

➤ That there is nothing better than hearing from others how they handle what we stumble over. In one instance, we were asked to help in a situation where a remodeler who sold extremely high-end projects to the well-to-do would leave the first meeting and tell the prospects to call if they wanted to proceed.

In giving advice, we had to take into account his clients and his selling style but we were able to work through a scenario he was comfortable with that invited the client to the next step and yet didn't make him feel too pushy.

➤ It was clear that most of us have a selling style that tends to remain the same but that our buyers have a number of different buying styles. If we are highly detailed in our selling, we will appeal to the engineer type but we will bore the creative and style-oriented prospect who may not want to hear all the details. So it was really interesting to hear from a table of remodelers (with differing buying styles) as to what they would want to know and hear. Somehow, the seller has to elicit clues about how the prospect wants to buy.

➤ Some of the "demonstrators" were somewhat weak on questioning and listening for cues as to what the underlying motivation for the project was (the pain), who was the decision-maker, what budget range would satisfy, what previous experience with remodeling the prospect had had (and with what outcome), what factors (budget, design, remodeler reputation) would influence the decision, and when the project needed to be signed (or designed) in order to meet the prospect's timeline.

There is so much the professional remodeler must communicate to differentiate themselves from the everyday contractor that sometimes listening to the prospect can take a back seat.

And there was much, much more. Try this crazy role-playing. You'll be surprised what you learn and how fast you learn it.

51-Percenters

In this era of best-selling business books that are novels with lessons, why not read the exciting *true* story of a 27-year-old who conquered the stratospheric world of New York City fine dining? Danny Meyer came with lots of baggage, including a father who grew his two businesses into bankruptcy—a fact that would both haunt him and teach him some valuable lessons.

The book is *Setting the Table: The Transforming Power of Hospitality in Business*, written by Danny Meyer, owner of unique signature restaurants, including Union Square Café, Gramercy Tavern, Eleven Madison Park, Tabla, and Blue Smoke. So what does a restaurateur have to teach a remodeler? Lots, because the businesses share many similarities.

Both restaurants and remodelers provide a service wrapped around a product. The upscale client's delight or disappointment depends on both the service and the product being impeccable. That service takes lots of good-natured and technically proficient staff to deliver well. The failure rates in both businesses top the charts. Both businesses—at the high end—are resistant to replication. In both, success depends on repeat clients and great word-of-mouth referrals.

There is so much to learn from Meyer's story.

> ➤ His restaurants have a unique selling proposition (USP). No two restaurants are the least bit alike except that all, according to Meyer's mission statement, "express excellence in the most inclusive, accessible, genuine, and hospitable way possible."
>
> Each restaurant has its own niche but updates whatever concept or type of food it offers. While most are fine dining, Meyer developed the "Shake Shack" for burgers and shakes in Central Park and clients wait in long lines to buy the superior food. Whatever area Meyer touches—park snacks, museum food, or barbecue—he works to transform it and take it to a higher level.
>
> So his niche, his USP, is not a type of food or a type of restaurant but unexpectedly better food, delivered in a very special and friendly way. What is your USP, your distinctive strategy that puts you out of reach of your competitors?
>
> ➤ Meyer has developed a simple but clearly defined and frequently com-

municated philosophy of doing business. His restaurants are based on the philosophy of "enlightened hospitality." He defines service as "the technical delivery of a product" and hospitality as, "how the delivery of that product makes its recipient *feel*." Enlightened hospitality requires a dialogue—that is, being on the diner's side. He writes, "To be on the guest's side requires listening to that person with every sense, and following up with a thoughtful, gracious, and appropriate response."

➤ Hiring and training to support this philosophy of hospitality is critical. The delivery of enlightened hospitality must be on the spot by staff. Training can deliver the principles and guidelines, but each worker has to have a positive attitude and good judgment to deliver as the occasion calls for it. Meyer is firm that this hospitality must begin with how his staff members treat each other and only then will it shine forth to include the guests.

➤ "The only way a company can grow, stay true to its soul, and remain consistently successful is to attract, hire, and keep great people. It's that simple, and it's that hard," Meyer says. He wants "51-percenters." A perfect employee would get 49% of their final 100% score on technical proficiency and 51% for their innate emotional skills for hospitality because "training for emotional skills is next to impossible." He also tries to hire only candidates who will eventually place in the top three all-time hires in their category.

"To me, a 51-percenter has five core emotional skills," says Meyer. "Optimistic warmth, intelligence, work ethic, empathy, self-awareness, and integrity."

➤ Success generates opportunities. Deals constantly come to Meyer now that he has proven his philosophy, processes, and systems. He turns down 15 opportunities for every one he accepts. He is looking for context. "What has guided me most as an entrepreneur is the confluence of passion and opportunity (and sometimes serendipity) that leads to the right context for the right idea at the right time in the right place and for the right value," he writes. He maintains that he has made more money by saying no than by saying yes.

There's lots more to be gleaned from this excellent read. As I read Meyer's fast-moving tale, I wanted to be in New York trying out each of his restaurants and experiencing each from the diner's perspective. If you happen to be a foodie, you will have double the pleasure from this book. Bon appetit!

A Dream With a Date Attached

Most remodelers give current clients some sort of holiday gift as a thank-you for business. But Michael Spreckelmeier, owner of Progressive Builders, Inc., in Ft. Myers, Fla., has elevated this tradition to a whole new level. His system maximizes the company culture by including others in the customizing of gifts for each client and personal delivery wherever possible. He then builds on that with a goal-setting session with staff and a heart-warming team building exercise. Here's how he rolls all these achievements into the simple act of holiday gift-giving.

"We purchase wholesale fruit, buy beautiful baskets, shop for high-quality chocolates, coffee, and, if the clients have pets, a gift for each pet," explains Spreckelmeier. In mid-December his staff fans out and hand delivers the baskets. "Some clients actually freak out when I am delivering their basket," he says. "I just tell them I can't deliver all the baskets, but that it is important for me to deliver this one." But that is only the beginning.

The staff reassembles at the company office, where they review the year just ending and their accomplishments. Then they turn their attention to the upcoming year. It is time for personal and professional goal setting "to help extract the true thoughts and dreams of our team," says Spreckelmeier. He hands out a two-page sheet for them to fill out on the spot.

He defines a goal as "a dream with a date attached," and the form asks them to set their goals for the new year. Why not have the staff come to the meeting having filled out the form? Spreckelmeier finds that some forget and that doing it on the spot is more effective. Last year's goals are reviewed and goals are publicly declared for the upcoming year.

Next, it's on to strengths and weaknesses with an emphasis on the former. At Progressive, it's done in a pleasant and diplomatic fashion. Each person thinks of what they could do at work to improve their value to the team. Everyone's name is put in a box. "This step is where it can and does get crazy," says Spreckelmeier.

He draws a name from the box, announces it, and praises the person whose name he just drew. There are rules for praising. It can last no more than 20 seconds and it can't suggest improvement or use the word "but." After the public praising, the employee must say, "Thank you, and I agree with you," and then must add "but…." and tell the group in 20 seconds what they plan to improve on the next year.

"This exercise is a blast," the remodeler says. "As this unrolls, I've been able to remember the first job they worked on, or the date they started, or something personal." He is also a fan of using handwritten cards to employees throughout the year to praise them for something they have taught, learned, or improved. The card will contain a check and a special message like, "Our company is blessed to have you on our team," "Thank you for your dedication to excellence," and "Look how far we have come together."

There's still time for each of us to be creative in our holiday traditions. So don't just deliver holiday gifts; build this act of generosity into a process that will inspire both your clients and your team

Gifts to Give All Year

'Tis the season when most of us better get shopping! I don't know about you but I hate shopping, so I have assembled a list of purchase-less gifts to give some of the important people in your life. These are listed in no particular order:

For Your Company and Staff

Vision. Give them an inspiring picture of what the company can be and what purpose it can serve that is bigger than just the company. Keep talking about it. Compare every action and plan against it to be sure you are heading in the right direction.

The A Team. Do you have any B or C players? Do you tolerate B or C performance? If so, the A players may get discouraged and leave. Commit to building on a first-class foundation of the right people in the right places.

Double the Fun. Whatever you are doing now for fun—summer picnic, holiday party, white-water rafting, celebrations at the end of each big job, birthday parties—double it. Why not appoint a cross-departmental committee and give them some funds to plan next year's fun get-togethers?

For Yourself

Time for an activity or hobby you really love. For my eldest son, it's agility training and competition for his two rescue shelties. For my younger son, it's long bike rides early on Sunday morning. Everyone is counting on you, so you need to nurture yourself.

Separation between your personal success and company success. Maybe your company isn't doing so well. It's depressing, but you are still a great person. Maybe your company is doing superbly. Watch out for bloated self-esteem and arrogance. Remember the old-but-true reminder that no one ever was remembered by those they love for their business successes.

Over 50? Give yourself, your family, and your company an exit strategy. Your company has value. How can you make the most of it?

For Your Family

Your time, your love, and your attention. Do a reality check here. Could you do better? If so, how would you do better?

Financial security. No matter what stage of life you are at, a financial plan from a fee-only financial planner will help you see what it will take to achieve your goals when you want to achieve them. It may be college for the kids, retirement for you and your spouse, and that long-awaited trip to Italy. Let's get serious about this.

For Your Community

Time and/or money. Isn't Rosa Parks an incredible example of what one person can do and can change? Remodelers are powerful, action-oriented people. What can you do to help? What can you change?

For Everybody in Your Life

Double your sincere praise. It's free, it's easy, and it's incredibly powerful. But it means you'll focus on catching people doing things right. Watch them bloom.

Maybe none of these gift ideas hit exactly the right note, but you get the idea. There is so much you can give those around you (and yourself) that never requires going to a mall.

chapter four

MANAGING TO THE MAX

Creating a Structure of
Governance that Works

How to Make Money in Remodeling

Meetings, Meetings, Meetings

Death by Meeting

Accidents Happen—Frequently!

Systematically Systematizing

Accountability—the Ultimate
Hot Button

More Accountability

And Still More on Accountability

Continuously Improving

Now Hear This

> *"Management means,
> in the last analysis,
> the substitution of
> thought for brawn
> and muscle, of
> knowledge for folklore
> and superstition,
> and of cooperation
> for force...."*
>
> **Peter Drucker**

AGAIN AND AGAIN, as I consult with remodeling companies, I recommend the same action to cure many of their ills. And again and again, they report major improvements when they follow this relatively simple advice. The problem is that many of the companies have outgrown their management structure and yet have staff on board—who, if mobilized by the right structure—can help lead the company.

Author Michael Gerber (*The E Myth*) writes of the critical need to not only work IN your company but to work ON the company as well. Gerber stresses that every company—no matter how small—needs both big-picture and day-to-day governing. Most owners manage to get the day-to-day on the schedule, but they often miss the critical big-picture planning and monitoring. Most staff are never engaged in working ON the company.

Creating a Structure of Governance that Works

As companies grow, they need a more formal governing system—one that is multi-level. It is no longer enough to run the company by chatting as you pass another person's desk or to write them e-mails. You need more consistent and reliable ways to communicate information and make decisions, take on tasks, and report back progress. You also begin to need high-level strategic planning and monitoring that you may not have needed earlier in your company development. And you need to involve more of your staff in decision making and monitoring the results.

Here are four levels of authority and accountability that make sense for companies over $1 million. If your company is smaller, simplify this structure to what will work for you.

> ➤ First establish a board of directors. Your board will be composed of yourself and any other partners as well as key management team members (head of sales, production, administration) and anyone else who will contribute effectively and with whom you feel comfortable sharing any information about the company—good or bad. The board of directors will meet quarterly or monthly and discuss only the highest level, big-picture issues and planning. They approve the budget and business goals, make course corrections, and approve any major business decisions.

> ➤ Next, develop your key management team as a management force on your behalf. Thus, the head of sales, production, and administration will meet with you on a weekly basis for a meeting that is likely to last 90 minutes. There will be a formalized report from each attendee as well as a chance to get input on the challenges each is facing.
>
> One person will keep notes to be distributed to each attendee after the meeting. This is a "state of the company" update and lets everyone in on just how the company is doing, what actions need to be taken, and who is to do what by when.

> ➤ On a weekly basis, each department head will meet with their staff to reiterate departmental objectives and find out how each job, sale, or administrative task is going. Again, goals are set and monitored and challenges are addressed at this departmental level. As owner, you will

visit occasionally as an observer but the department head will run these meetings.

➤ Meet with the entire staff on an annual, semi-annual, or quarterly basis. This is your chance as owner to communicate a uniform message about where the company is going, what your vision for the company is, and where your major goals are taking you.

Set an unvarying schedule of meetings each week. They occur every week, no matter what. There is no option to cancel them. These meetings are the first thing to be placed on each month's schedule. And be sure to keep the meetings on time and on track.

This structure trains tomorrow's leaders for your company and unifies the company direction and goals. It will save time from those informal communications and certainly enhances accountability. By setting your key goals and then getting every level of the company to attack them, you'll be amazed by the momentum you achieve. You will be harnessing the true power of your company.

How to Make Money in Remodeling

Here is a well-known joke: How do you make a million dollars in remodeling? Start with $3 million! Well, we'd rather make real money in this business to fund the life of our family, that of our employees' families, and the future growth of the company.

The simple (but not easy) answer is to just live within your means from a business perspective. If you believe that you can only earn $50,000 or $100,000 in gross profit, then you have to use only three-quarters of that figure in overhead, including your salary. Or, to put it another way, the company must consistently take in more than it spends.

But How?

It just won't happen unless you are an owner who believes that making money involves even more than satisfying clients and building beautiful projects. It is the result of those in combination with the good financial management of your company. You must *make it happen.* That means you must watch the piggy bank—in other words, understand and focus on those all important financial reports.

Set up two key financial "loops" in your business. In a loop, you make a financial plan, you monitor that plan by gathering information in a useful format, and you adapt your actions to straighten out any variances and return to the beginning—replan, regather, readapt, etc. The big-picture loop is about the overall company operation. The smaller picture loop focuses on job costs, the most unpredictable of your expenditures.

The Big-Picture Loop

Here, you are creating a feedback loop that includes the development of at least one operational budget for the year, which integrates the following components:

➤ your realistically anticipated volume

➤ the gross profit percentage you plan to achieve

➤ a line-item budget for your overhead that shows that you will have a net profit of 8 to 10% after all expenses.

This budget is then broken down into monthly numbers.

That's your plan. You then gather information monthly that shows budget to actual (your P&L,) a common report format in all accounting software. This allows you to take quick action if you are getting off track.

Here are some key ingredients:

➤ Accurate financial reports—P&L and balance sheet in an approved format for remodelers—COGS and estimating categories in perfect sync.

➤ These financial reports are based on percent of completion accounting.

➤ Realistic annual budget for company monitored monthly.

➤ Adapted (re-balanced) as needed or at least quarterly.

➤ Entered into the accounting system so a monthly estimate-to-actual report can be generated and monitored.

➤ Budget and financials planned and shared with everyone—or at least key team members—so that they buy in to the recipe for success. Wherever possible, key line items like office supplies, insurance, and job costs have a "champion" who will be responsible and accountable for bringing them in at or below budget.

The Small-Picture Loop

This loop is all about estimating and job costing. Some of your jobs will come in well, some not. Successful remodelers create an overall consistency by bringing jobs in within 2% of estimates, but only in the aggregate. They, too, have individual jobs that are over or under estimates.

Here again to make money you need a plan (your estimate), reporting against that plan (job-cost reports weekly or bi-weekly), and analysis of why a job may be over or under. Do we need to adjust our estimating? Do we need better job performance? Are we handing off well from whoever sold the job to production?

Here are some key ingredients for the job-cost feedback loop:

➤ Formatted estimates understandable by everyone

➤ Trade contractors provide fixed-price bids and must notify company of any change before undertaking it

➤ Estimates checked by production manager or knowledgeable second person in company

➤ Estimates entered into accounting system

➤ Job-cost information gathered in same categories as estimates

➤ Biweekly or weekly job-cost reports showing estimate to actual are generated

➤ These reports are studied and monitored by leads, project managers, or production managers. Company places high emphasis on bringing jobs in on or below budget

➤ Change orders—written and collected upfront with standard markup.

➤ Draws—well constructed to favor the company and promptly collected with only a small draw remaining as last payment.

The Result

Creating and maximizing these two loops in your company allows you to adjust operations to land your company plane on the carrier deck of profitability. Without them, you are flying blind.

Meetings, Meetings, Meetings...

Meetings. Are they time-wasters, money-squanderers, gripe sessions, and ill-planned interruptions to actually getting work done? That's what many remodelers think. Consequently, they don't hold formal meetings even in multi-million dollar companies.

I disagree. Well-run meetings harness your team to achieve goals and to be accountable for results in their day-to-day roles. They allow an owner to communicate a uniform message efficiently and build future leaders for the company.

Picture such a meeting. It's the weekly Key Management Team meeting. It is *always* held Tuesdays at 8 a.m. It includes the company owner, the office manager, the sales manager, and the production manager.

Everyone has learned to be there on time because they know the meeting will start right at 8 and they will be embarrassed to walk in late. They know that it will end by 9:30 a.m. and have scheduled their day accordingly. There are no interruptions for answering phone calls, etc., unless it is a true emergency. The meeting is facilitated by the company owner working from a written agenda. If the company owner is on vacation, the meeting is run by one of the Key Team.

The office manager has e-mailed the agenda to everyone before the meeting. She compiles it by checking with each attendee as to whether they have an issue they want to discuss, how much time should be allotted to that issue, and how high a priority it is (just in case there is too much on the agenda.) She arranges the agenda with departmental reports first, ongoing project reports next (they are working on streamlining the handoff from sales to production and each attendee has some "homework" they've agreed to bring to the next meeting), and new issues last.

She also makes sure the flash report—a concise, one-page report with key data—has been compiled and copied for each attendee. It includes leads taken in, sales made, jobs closed, client evaluation scores received, and much more. The Key Team finds that having this information pre-packaged for the meeting saves considerable time and keeps them focused on the important numbers they want to track.

Once a month, analyzing the latest P&L and balance sheet is on the agenda as well as reviewing the company's budget-to-actual report. This meeting is 2 hours long because the Key Team's goal for the year is to get better educated about how to read financials and use the information they provide to manage better. To train themselves, they read and discuss a chapter in a book on financial management for non-financial people and their friendly neighborhood accountant comes in to answer questions and teach a short lesson.

As the meeting progresses, the office manager takes notes on what has been agreed upon and who will do what by when. These notes will be e-mailed to all attendees and the agreements of what will be done by the next meeting are rolled forward into that new agenda.

The facilitator keeps the meeting on task and on time and asks participants who might have gotten off track to work on that later, outside the meeting. Everyone leaves the meeting updated on the state of the entire company and with a sense of accomplishment that they are invested in the company's success and that the company is continuously improving.

Yes, this is the picture of the perfect meeting! But the point is that great meetings don't just happen—they are the result of organization and planning. If your meetings are floundering, make them productive with these seven tools:
- ➤ A clear purpose
- ➤ Guidelines for behavior
- ➤ Written agenda
- ➤ Defined time frame
- ➤ Facilitator
- ➤ Minutes
- ➤ Flash report—Pre-meeting information gathering

And don't forget to throw in some fun, celebration, and recognition. You will make good meetings even better.

Death by Meeting

How could you not be compelled to read a book called *Death by Meeting*?

We've all experienced mind-and body-numbing meetings when we couldn't wait to be released to do our "real work."

But if you assume that author Patrick Lencioni is going to recommend dropping all meetings, you'll be disappointed. He's actually a fan of meetings—the right kind of meetings. Lencioni just wants you to change the type and frequency and length of your meetings. And—hold onto your hat—he wants you to add drama to meetings—to make them more like movies! But I'm getting ahead of myself.

The book is formatted (as was his excellent earlier book—*The Five Dysfunctions of a Team*) in two sections. The first is a fictional story of a caring but less-than-effective CEO and how well-structured meetings saved his job. Unlike most books that have overly simplified fables, this story is well written and interesting. The second section is an explanation of the theory of meetings being taught by the fable. So you actually can bypass the fiction and go right to the meat of the business teaching if that is your preference.

Four types of company meetings are recommended for your key management team. The first is a daily check-in or huddle conducted standing up and lasting only 5 minutes. This is a chance for your key managers to share their three main priorities for the day. The second type of meeting is the weekly tactical meeting lasting 45 to 90 minutes to review weekly priorities. Both of these meetings are very short term in outlook.

The third type is a monthly strategic meeting of 2 to 4 hours, where the focus is those issues (limited to a maximum of two topics) affecting the long-term success of the business. The last is a quarterly off-site review of 1 to 2 days that is very big-picture and might review company strategy, team development, incentive programs, etc.

Lencioni's ideas for the weekly tactical meeting seem particularly innovative. He recommends starting with a lightning round in which each attendee (usually your management team) has no more than 60 seconds to list their priorities for the week. Next, the key metrics that spell success for the company are reviewed. There should be no more than six and the review should take no more than 5 minutes.

The book's most revolutionary recommendation is that there is to be no preplanned agenda for this meeting. The agenda is decided after the lightning round and metrics report. As Lencioni notes, "While this might mean sacrificing some control, it ensures that the meeting will be relevant and effective."

This set of meetings clearly separates priorities and issues of different scope and focus. There are meetings for short-term and long-term priorities. There are meetings to consider big-picture strategies and those for tactics. Otherwise, attendees are talking about plans for the picnic one minute and reviewing the marketing program or whether the company should open a second office the next. That's what Lencioni disparagingly brands as an ineffective "meeting stew."

But back to that drama that we are supposed to add to our meetings. That really is translated as healthy conflict. "Avoiding issues that merit debate and disagreement not only makes the meeting boring, it guarantees that the issues won't be resolved," writes Lencioni.

Thus, the leader of the meeting is encouraged to "mine" for conflict and get all opinions out on the table. Initially, that means watching for negative body language and encouraging that person to share their concerns. It means verbally praising a participant willing to disagree. Only by getting everyone's opinions on the table will the company end up with the best solution.

The best part of adding this drama to your meetings is that they become authentic and lively and worth attending. And you, and your Key Team, avoid that dreaded death by meeting.

Accidents Happen—Frequently!

I spent yesterday morning chasing down parts for a 1930's John Deere manure spreader and ordering seed for quail food plots. Ten years ago, if a gypsy fortune teller had foretold where I would be and how I would spend my personal and professional life today, I would have been incredulous.

Much of what we end up doing in life seems to be accidental and incapable of prediction. So when I came across a book titled *The Accidental Manager* (Gary S. Topchik, American Management Association, 2004), I sent for it. Most of us are accidental business owners, accidental leaders, and definitely accidental managers. We got into our fields of endeavor to do a job—not to manage and lead people.

Topchik defines managing as getting the work done through others by having them help you achieve the goals of the unit or organization. He defines leading as getting people to willingly do their jobs by providing the right type of personal environment for people to want to succeed. He notes that management is "more reactive and more operational, happening day to day," while leadership is "more proactive and future oriented." Organizations must have both to flourish.

While the book is directed at new managers being promoted (perhaps unwillingly) within a company, it has key messages for us all.

➤ Companies need to recognize that many top employees don't want to manage others. The employee often feels that they will have to make tough decisions and that the new duties will simply add to the duties they already have. However, if they are assured that a support and training system is in place, they will be more likely to make the change.

➤ Management usually is a learned skill and can and should be taught. This book is a great resource in doing just that.

➤ Companies need to recognize that an employee being promoted will have a lot to learn as they move to a managerial role. Topchik recommends that the promoted employee manage-only for the first few months so that they get a clear message of how important this role is and so that they have the time to do the managing.

Topchik covers what he calls the four platinum behaviors that transform an accidental manager into a successful manager:

➤ The ability to develop staff, including effective delegating and training that supports that development.

➤ The ability to listen actively for meaning and understanding and to let the other person know that they have been heard.

➤ The ability to give and receive feedback. He discusses five types of feedback, how to deliver both positive and constructive feedback, and how to receive feedback from team members.

➤ The ability to create a motivational climate that encourages staff to motivate themselves. Here, Topchik gives 15 strategies for firing up employees to work as a team toward organizational goals.

Any remodeler who feels challenged by managing people—and who doesn't? —would benefit from the user-friendly information in this book. The author includes a self-administered 50-question assessment to get you started.

Why not be proactive and develop a management training group that uses the book as a text with perhaps a chapter a month assigned and then discussion at the monthly meeting with a homework exercise? Then, when you ask your top salesperson to consider becoming sales manager, you both understand the challenge and the transitions. Or when you consider your top lead carpenter for the new position of production manager, you can discuss the management aspects of the job with clarity.

Systematically Systematizing

How do we transform the raw-material new hire into the superstar of tomorrow? It's simple but certainly not easy. That transformation occurs when two key elements are in place in our company—culture and systems.

First, we immerse the new hire in our meaningful company *culture* that teaches the company's core values and encourages and rewards the right behavior.

Then we support them with *systems* designed to help them produce the desired results time after time—predictably. Author Michael Gerber, in his seminal work *The E Myth,* calls a system a completely predictable technology for producing desired results which were formerly unpredictable. So let's talk systems in your business.

Systems, systems, systems—we all want them…right now! But do we really understand what they are, what they will do for us, and how to develop them and put them in place?

What is a business system and what will its benefits be? It is, the dictionary says, a procedure or process for obtaining an objective. The conglomerate of all your systems forms the way you do business. Standardizing the way you do business is key to growing your company.

Otherwise, each new hire will bring their systems to the company and you will have a mish-mash of what works and what doesn't and a lot of non-alignment between systems. Then when that person leaves, a new hire with new systems arrives and you have a company that doesn't look like what you envision and doesn't deliver what you believe must be delivered to the client.

Systems that work are extremely valuable. Most franchises charge a lot of money for a set of systems that is already developed and hopefully proofed. That's why buyers look for a franchise that has some units in operation—to make sure the business format really does work.

Here are six tips for systematizing your company:

ONE: Make sure there is a fit between the complexity of your systems and your company size. If you have a 3-person company, your systems will be much simpler than those for a 30-person company. That's because the most error-prone areas of a business are the handoffs between one person and another.

The single system we hear the most groans about is the sales-to-production handoff. Or, if the salesperson is different from the estimator in your company, considerable information must be transferred between the two and verbal communication really won't work. Thus are born checklists and forms and a system.

Another example of a system is your time card for field workers, which carries written information between the worker and the bookkeeper so that an accurate paycheck gets written, accurate job costs are generated, and estimating can be kept updated.

TWO: Create your highly systematized company one puzzle piece at a time. Pick the areas where getting organized and developing procedures will give you the highest impact. Eventually, you'll have the whole puzzle filled out and everything will connect. Don't try to do too much at once. Each new system has to have time and focus to turn it into a habit.

THREE: Once you identify the need for a system to solve a conflict (the result being delivered isn't the result you want to have), try to research how other companies have handled the same issue. See if other remodelers will share their system with you.

FOUR: Get an interdepartmental team on the job. You might be tempted to quietly develop a system by yourself and then excitedly unveil it to a notably un-excited staff. You saved time in development, but now you have the Herculean task of getting buy-in.

Instead, toss the ball to your team. Be sure representatives of every part of the staff that will be affected are on that team. Let them do the research and design the system, making sure it will work for all stakeholders (clients, staff, suppliers, and subs). Then they will be anxious to implement it because they are sold on the benefits.

FIVE: Execute successfully. Designing a system is child's play compared to the discipline of implementing it and making it habitual. This is where most companies lose it. Not only that but sometimes—of course not in *your* company—company owners are the first to drop the use of a system. That's a killer. If you don't walk your talk, no one else will, either. This is the stage that will test your determination and commitment.

The important issue here is whether your company has learned to apply an agreed-upon system and stick with it through thick and thin. There will be days that you and they feel too busy—or a project or issue seems not to need to be put through all the steps. That is when you are tested and that is when it is most important that your systems are respected.

SIX: Systematizing is an endless journey, not a destination. Your systems will need revisiting with the passage of time, with the addition of staff, or with the changing of departments. You'll know because you will begin to see errors creep in and feel that conflict that develops when the results obtained don't match the vision.

Remember—a journey of a thousand miles (systematization) starts with but a single step....

Accountability–the Ultimate Hot Button

If there's a hot, hot, hot button among remodelers, it is accountability and how to achieve it. There's a constant outcry of "why can't my employees be responsible for what they promise? for what we require? for following our systems? for getting it done on time or on budget?"

Accountability is "A personal choice to … demonstrate the ownership necessary for achieving desired results," say the authors of *The Oz Principle: Getting Results Through Individual and Organizational Accountability.* Wikipedia defines this key trait as the acknowledgement and assumption of responsibility for actions and decisions, including the obligation to report, explain, and be answerable for the resulting consequences.

Both of these definitions seem to put the emphasis on the individual. And it's probable that you will not morph an employee who shows no acceptance of responsibility in his/her personal life into a highly accountable hire. At the same time, you can hire folks who are willing to take responsibility and not give them the structure or the culture needed to make accountability work.

"People who have the ability to organize their own lives seem to have a higher likelihood of helping me keep my business family in order," says Ty Melton of Melton Construction Inc., in Boulder, Colo. Melton has been emphasizing the building of an accountability culture for several years. "Some people have never worked at a company like ours with goals, meetings, and job descriptions," he says. "The right employee thrives on having a compass and resetting and achieving goals."

Melton's push for accountability centers on a monthly goals meeting. Here's how he describes the format: "All hands show up. We start promptly. I give a brief overview of the state of the company. Then we review goals department by department. For instance, our marketing goal is $600,000 worth of leads each month. Sales, and also design, are responsible for keeping $1.2 million of work in backlog—4 months work for our company.

"Estimating is focused on a specific gross profit and a second goal of having a complete handoff package as graded by the production manager.

Production has the hardest job in the company because they are responsible for three metrics. Jobs must be completed on time as measured by a spreadsheet, on budget as measured by our gross profit, and with happy clients as measured by our satisfaction survey. "

If a department is having difficulty meeting their goals, the participants have a lightning round of getting input from each person at the meeting who is to offer help or a suggestion as to how they can get back on track. Then the department representative says which of the ideas they plan to utilize.

With his goals meetings, Melton has built in some of the key components to making accountability the company standard:

➤ He understands that accountability thrives in the right company *culture.*

➤ He has clear *metrics* for the success or failure in each department and those metrics are tied to key success indicators in the company plan.

➤ He has involved the *team* to help put pressure on each department to do its part.

➤ When the ball is dropped, Melton encourages team members to *help* each other refocus on achieving the goal.

➤ Accountability includes *consequences.* The team can come down on you, the boss can come down on you, and, ultimately, you can work elsewhere.

Melton stresses how accountability works for everyone on his team. "We have the goals meetings to create a stable, less-stressful work environment," he says. "If each one of us does our own part, we will all succeed."

More Accountability

What can we learn about accountability in business from Donald Trump's reality-television approach to finding his next executive? Trump's version of the game of business includes being part of a team where you try never to take responsibility and indeed where you may even undermine the team performance in order to protect yourself. The participants will throw teammates under the bus to survive. And, most importantly, we learn that a small mistake will get you called on the carpet before millions of people and is likely to get you "fired."

That perspective on accountability is just plain wrong. If you examine accountability in top remodeling companies, you learn a completely different form of taking responsibility—one that encourages everyone in the company to happily accept responsibility for realistic results, and one that is more about praise than blame.

I interviewed seven remodelers I particularly admire in search of their wisdom on accountability. While there was universality in their understanding of what accountability is and how critically important it is in delivering predictably excellent service to their clients, they each had a different take on how they integrated it into their company. The following six accountability "truths" synthesize their methods:

➤ Walk your talk. Owners must *model* personal and organizational accountability. It's not unusual to hear remodelers say they wish they could follow the company systems like they expect others to, but that their roles are just too all-consuming. Or they wish they could always hold meetings at the agreed-upon time and day but they have too many conflicts.

➤ All seven remodelers quashed this "it-doesn't-apply-to-me" thinking and agreed that their willingness to follow the rules, be on time, follow through on commitments, and publicly admit their failures was key to holding others accountable. "I find myself fighting to follow our systems but I am committed to them," says David Foster of Foster Remodeling Solutions.

➤ Think big and think long term. Accountability is a *culture* that is grown and developed over the years in a company. As Jim Strite of Strite Design + Remodel chuckles, "It only took us 16 years to get to this place." Is your company one in which the staff and operations encourage commitment, the taking of responsibility, and the delivering of results? Would a new hire quickly understand that to fit in and remain with the company they will have to deliver?

➤ Careful *hiring* is the key. You want employees who have demonstrated accountability in their personal and work lives. An Atlanta remodeler says, "I'm not good at managing people who aren't accountable, so I have to hire accountable people." During the prospect's interview and the checking of references, be sure to include questions that hone in on the candidate's willingness to make reasonable commitments and be responsible for results. This due diligence should include a background check for criminal convictions and driving violations as well as drug testing.

➤ As Michael Gerber, author of *The E Myth* espouses, "Systems run your company. People run your systems." The development of *systems* and the adherence to their use is key to accountability. Systems represent tried-and-true processes that produce success. They are one of the most valuable entities a company has. Yet in many companies, systems exist but are used only intermittently by staff.

➤ Set inspiring and significant *goals* and create *metrics* that clearly show your progress. Make a direct connection between each individual's job and those goals and assign key metrics to measure their ability to deliver results.

➤ "Some people have never worked at a company like ours, with goals meetings, and job descriptions," explains Ty Melton of Melton Construction. "They thrive on having a compass and resetting and achieving goals."

➤ Feedback is the breakfast of champion businesses and it's one of the secrets to building an accountable workforce and company. Publicly communicated metrics show every individual and team how they are doing. Be sure to reward aligned behavior and counsel non-aligned employees.

➤ For Iris Harrell of Harrell Remodeling, creating feedback loops is an accountability must-do. "I resisted job costing for years because I was afraid it would be a punishment session" she says. "But we set the tone with we're going to learn from this and we're going to share what we've learned. The culture of our job-costing meeting is that you share mistakes, not hide them. If you don't (and the owner has to do the same) how can you get better?"

Experts say the strongest and most powerful enforcer of accountability is the team and only secondarily is the owner. In a culture of accountability, the weak, the unwilling, and the irresponsible are soon exposed and can be freed up to work for your competitors.

And Still More on Accountability

Much that is written and spoken about accountability focuses on personal accountability. In their book *The Oz Principle: Getting Results Through Individual and Organizational Accountability*, authors Roger Connors, Tom Smith, and Craig Hickman define accountability as "a personal choice to rise above one's circumstances and demonstrate the ownership necessary for achieving desired results."

But most remodelers want to know how to create an organizational culture of accountability. To succeed at establishing accountability does mean creating an all-pervasive culture that emphasizes and rewards taking responsibility for results. Let's look at how Jay Van Deusen of Van Deusen Construction Company in Bel Air, Md., uses detailed job descriptions linked with metrics and coupled with prioritization of duties to drive accountability in his organization.

For Van Deusen, accountability means "trying to get everybody to know what their job is rather than trying to infer it so they can make themselves successful in our company in their role with very clear ways to measure that success."

So how does it work? Well, if you are the bookkeeper at the Van Deusen company, your job description contains only three sections but each section is linked to metrics. Accounting and business administration constitutes 60% of the job, office assisting duties are 23%, and human resources is 17%. The description of work under accounting and business administration is:

"Accounting and administration provide the tools to judge where the profitability of the company lies. Accurate and knowledgeable, the bookkeeper thoroughly understands basic accounting principles and can apply them to ensure the financial accuracy of the construction company, including: General Accounting, A/P, A/R, Job Costing Reports, WIP reports, Property Management Activities, and other reporting instruments. The bookkeeper works with the General Manager, the corporate accountant, and administration manager to provide accurate reporting."

There's nothing radical there, but the next paragraph spells out what will constitute success in this area.

"Success in this area is critical to the company. Satisfactory rating for accuracy of entries and understanding of accounting principles by the General Manager, Production Manager, Administration Manager, and corporate accountant of 87% or better. This rating is achieved with the results of a survey from each member above."

Thus, the job description sets up the ability to produce a numerically scored performance review. And each employee knows just how they will be graded and what the report card is for their job. Van Deusen conducts performance reviews at 30, 60 and 90 days for new employees and semi-annually for other staff. The review report is a spreadsheet. The employee ranks themselves in each area, and then they are ranked by the surveys from each person described in their job description. All the rankings are melded onto one percentage; for the bookkeeper, that percentage must be 87% or higher.

For instance, if the production manager ranks the bookkeeper as doing 93% of their accounting function and that represents 60% of their duties, (.93 x 60 = 55.8), they receive 55.8% toward the total score. There is room on the review sheet for notes and comments are added during the session.

The performance review also includes an important section on 11 behaviors that the company has identified as key to company-wide success. These, too, are given weighting and are scored.

They include:
1. Do you write it down?
2. Do you do what you say you are going to do when you say you are going to do it?
3. Do you suggest alternatives for problem solving?
4. Are you visibly satisfied with your job?
5. Are you on time for the work day?

Van Deusen has found the system, developed with a consultant, helps him to be clear and objective in describing roles and in evaluating them and coaching his staff to set goals for improvement. While he's still in the early stages of this transition, his approach makes a lot of sense both for your staff and your ability to focus everyone on the important and to give them concise feedback as to how they are doing.

Continuously Improving

When Carroll Bogard, marketing manager for remodeling and replacement at Pella Corporation, invited me to take Pella's Continuous Improvement class, I jumped at the chance. It's a course that is given monthly for employees of all types and levels and it's the lead-in to Pella's more advanced Kaizen series of courses.

The warmth, fun, and exuberant learning in the classroom far overshadowed the zero-degree Iowa weather with snow and ice and blustery winds. There were perhaps 16 attendees, including some of Pella's suppliers, and we were quickly immersed in a whirlwind day that combined short bursts of learning about lean manufacturing based on the Toyota Production System and four longer segments where we formed a team focused on building three models of paper airplanes. Our goal was to rework a very bulky and chaotic manufacturing line to one that would reliably produce a quality plane every 15 seconds.

After a quick introduction to lean manufacturing, the attendees would go to another room to manufacture planes for 10 minutes and then convene to appoint a manager who would help us brainstorm better ways to reduce waste, reduce labor, reconfigure our working areas, and more—all focused on high-quality, low waste. Nothing was off limits.

However, our "manager" then had to convince the "factory owner," (played by a staff person) to let his team try out their ideas. The owner was not quick to accept change and inevitably the negotiations would end with permission to try some of our ideas but hold the line on others—very real world. In the end, our team reconfigured the work space, reduced inventory, filled customer orders on time, and redistributed what had been eight people's work to only four people. And success was ours as planes came off the line every 15 seconds.

While the Toyota Production System is about lean manufacturing, there are some key principles that can clearly apply to remodeling:

> ➤ Look at continuous improvement as a philosophy that must be fully embraced at every level over a long period of time if it is to work. It is not a Band-Aid solution. It must be embedded in the culture of a company. It must be lived by every employee. The potential rewards are huge.

➤ Encourage every worker to rethink, reengineer, and improve their own processes with help from their coworkers. It was abundantly clear in our group of 16 that each person, whether from bookkeeping or a factory floor, had great ideas to contribute as long as the environment was welcoming and safe. Often, the best ideas came from an unexpected person who worked in another area. Our success was definitely team success and could not have been done without input from all.

➤ Include suppliers and trade contractors in delivering on your quality and efficiency vision. We are only as good as our weakest link, and that weakest link may well be the plumber or the countertop company. Share your vision and your training with them.

➤ Encourage well-considered experiments. If you want to shorten lead-to-design time, dissect the steps and redesign and time the process on one job. You'll probably want to rework this another time and maybe another time until you have a system that gives you the speed and quality you are seeking.

➤ It may be simple, but clean work spaces and eliminating clutter improves focus, speed, and quality. We've been preaching clean, organized worksites for years—often as a client benefit—but there is a working advantage to be gained as well.

➤ Equally simple, consider layout in the office and on the job. If your bookkeeper has to walk 20 feet to the file cabinet, or if the office manager's printer is across the room, money and time are seeping out of your company unnoticed.

➤ Use visual read-outs and reports wherever possible and post them for all to contemplate. Our team was highly motivated by seeing that each iteration brought improvements in at least some of the key benchmarks we had to meet.

And don't forget to create a supportive culture that recognizes and rewards continuous improvements.

Now Hear This...

The waves of unhappy e-mails came rolling into my computer. "Why do we have to do this?" "Are you just making work for us?" "I'm too busy for 'home-work' that doesn't seem to lead anywhere." I was shocked. Two of us had worked really hard researching, discussing, and reading books to develop a meaningful homework package for a group of meetings this spring. There was a clear tie-in between their pre-meeting preparation and the meeting theme—but obviously only to the two of us. We had missed that all-important link: communication.

We had been so absorbed in the task, in the path that led us to believe that having our member clients do some upfront reading and best-practice preparation, that we'd forgotten to "sell" the benefits and simply rolled out the homework. When we realized what we had done, we apologized for our lapse and returned to that all-important communication. We communicated the linkage between the meeting preparation and having a more successful meeting and then everything proceeded smoothly.

Communication (or, really, the lack of) is one of the three big words we hear from our remodeler clients. The other two are accountability and leadership. While we all know what they mean, just complaining about them does not really define what the problem is. For instance, these were comments from employees in a recent consultation I did. When asked what could help them perform their jobs more effectively, they said:

➤ "Better communication"

➤ "If the owner communicated with me more about what the customer wants."

➤ "If we had better communication...now every decision has to be finalized by the owner."

It turned out that this company owner was trying to communicate the project details he learned during the sales process to his field crews as though his was a two- to three-person company. However, the company was now a 9- to 10-person company and although he had a production manager, he was bypassing him to issue short lead time changes directly to his field personnel. The right hand didn't know what the left hand was doing. For instance, the owner might be discussing a change of hardware with the homeowner while the field personnel were buying the original choice.

Gary Harpst has a wonderful chart in his recent book *Six Disciplines for Excellence: Building Small Businesses that Learn, Lead and Last.* He uses it to show that, "As organizations grow, communication challenges grow, as well; in fact they grow dramatically faster (exponentially) than the organization headcount does." The chart clearly shows that if your company consists of only three people, there are only three possible communication combinations (A and B, A and C, or B and C). Change your company to a 25-person company, an eight-fold increase in people, and there are 300 possible communication combinations. Communication complexity increases 100-fold!

If you are having what you would diagnose as communication challenges in your company, start by asking yourself these questions:

- ➤ Do I need a better system for communicating? As owner, should I be working through my key managers rather than around them?
- ➤ Am I writing down and distributing vital information like change orders?
- ➤ Could technology help me?
- ➤ Should I be holding more frequent meetings where everyone can get the same information at the same time (and where I can get their input)?
- ➤ Should I be holding better meetings with clear start and stop times and a substantive agenda that recognizes the company's communication needs?
- ➤ Am I forgetting to "sell" my ideas and changes? Am I connecting the dots as to what the benefits will be?
- ➤ Do I really have a safe environment for a give-and-take idea exchange? Can my personnel speak as freely to me as they do to that consultant I hired?

The playwright George Bernard Shaw once said, "The problem with communication…is the illusion that it has been accomplished." Let's banish that "illusion" part.

chapter five

PLANNING TO SUCCEED

The Long Term Plan

- The Foundation

- Where are You Coming From?

- Where are You Going?

Zoom In On Your 1-Year Plan

Some Thoughts on Marking Up

Want a Shorter Planning Process?

> *"Planning is an unnatural process; it is much more fun to do something. The nicest thing about not planning is that failure comes as a complete surprise, rather than being preceded by a period of worry and depression."*
>
> Sir John Harvey-Jones

L ET'S FACE IT—Some of us are into planning before doing and others are into diving in and doing. This section is all about planning with the understanding that it's cheap and easy to try things on paper before launching and very expensive and fraught with failure to launch without planning.

Even if you are an action-oriented remodeler, I bet you do a lot of planning (design, estimating, logistics, job file, etc.) before you start a job. Why? Because you know that thoughtful planning will help ensure your success. It's precisely the same in running your company. You need a plan to get you where you want to go.

In this section, we'll focus on two types of planning—long term (for the next 3 to 5 years) and short term (for the next year). If you're not working from a business plan now, try this approach and see if you don't find that it makes a significant difference in unifying the company, targeting your efforts, and gaining more ground. Let's start by planning the future and thinking longer term. Then we'll plan the next year and how much we can accomplish in heading toward those bigger future goals.

The Long Term Plan: Envisioning Your Future

A strategic business plan is not difficult to develop. You may have been scared off by 150-page plans concocted with consultants. Fat business plans tend to live on distant shelves, gathering dust. Rather, we are going to focus on a meaty, high-impact plan that takes three (yes, you read this right) pages. It will hit all the high points and will be much more accessible because it is short and to the point. But first, let's answer some key questions:

Why are we doing this?

These might be some of the reasons or you might have reasons of your own.

➤ To focus on what our goals need to be, to increase our focused drive to achieve well-thought-out goals. To increase our chance for success—as defined by us.

➤ To create a planning system/procedure in the company, a belief that future outcomes can be planned and implemented and that, because of that planning, they have a much greater chance of succeeding.

➤ To mobilize our team and unite them behind our goals through clear communication.

➤ To extend buy-in, responsibility, and accountability for success to every employee's job.

What kind of a plan is this?

There are business plans and business plans, so it is good to be clear about what kind of a plan this is and what it is meant to accomplish. What we are going to target is a plan for our internal company use, not for obtaining loans from a bank or investment from an investor. By making it an internal document, it can be concise and it can be real—not puffed up, not overly optimistic.

Who will be involved in the planning?

This is your decision; it's an important one. If you decide to go it alone and design your plan by yourself, then you've got to go out and "sell" it to your staff and that can be very time-consuming and difficult. Design it with your key staff and you will take more time upfront but then you have buy-in from the get-go. If you have a key management team established, definitely include them. Then they can communicate and motivate those who report to them to get on board.

What time frame should my plan cover?

It's not unusual to hear people talk about 10- and 20-year plans. Unless you have a very good reason to go longer (like retiring in 7 years), I would use a 3- to 5-year time frame. It's your choice.

Is there anything I should do before I start business planning?

Absolutely. You can do two important things:

First, develop and review your *personal life plan*. An entrepreneurial company has many reasons to exist, but the primary one is to support the owner's values, personal mission, and economic needs. At Remodelers Advantage, we define success as:

➤ above-average owner's compensation,

➤ a healthy net profit year after year,

➤ working hours that allow for a balanced life,

➤ the development of a significant company that delivers value to all stakeholders including employees, clients, trade contractors, and the community.

You may define success differently. The point is, define it for yourself and then be sure your business plan is in alignment with your personal mission, goals, values, and financial needs.

Second, daydream a bit. If you could look into a crystal ball and see yourself 5 years from now, what would really make you happy? What are you doing at the company? What does the company look like? What kinds of jobs and clients would you be specializing in? What kind of compensation would you be earning? Daydream the picture of where you want to be. As business guru Stephen Covey says, "Start with the end in mind."

Then review the last 5 years of your company's history. What has happened financially? What were the wins…and what were the losses? What is your company really good at? That information will help tremendously in how you want to plan the future. It will give you a sense of how far you currently are from where you want to be. Now let's pin things down on paper.

Section One: The Foundation

This page of your plan is about the rock upon which you have built your business—your *vision* for the future of your business, your *mission* or purpose for being in business, and the *core values* that will guide every action and decision. You may not have spelled these out before but you have lived them, modeled them to your staff, and based your praise and criticism on them.

But because they weren't spelled out, they couldn't be taught, you couldn't put them in job descriptions or policy manuals, and you didn't voice and communicate them. By thinking these three entities through, and by using them daily in your business, you will make them incredibly powerful in attracting good employees and keeping them and in running the business that you truly aspire to run. Notice that we're not doing this just so we can frame it and forget it. We are talking about making these three elements very real on a daily basis in your company and we will be aligning everything we do with them.

Step One: Vision. Let's get started. What is a vision statement? In his book, *Full Steam Ahead*, Ken Blanchard defines vision as "knowing who you are, where you are going, and what will guide your journey." A vision is an inspiring picture of the future you want—compelling, hard to reach, but worthy of moving toward. Typically, your vision will stay the same over many years.

A compelling vision will:
- ➤ Remind us what business we're really in.
- ➤ Provide guidelines that help us make daily decisions.
- ➤ Present a picture of the desired future that we can actually see.
- ➤ Be enduring, inspiring, and significant. It reaches the hearts and spirits of all your employees and helps each to see how he or she can contribute to something bigger than they are.

Here are some examples of compelling visions:
- ➤ Become a $125 billion company by 2000. (Walmart, 1990)
- ➤ Become number one or number two in every market we serve and revolutionize this company to have the strengths of a big company combined with the leanness and agility of a small company. (GE, 1980's)

➤ Crush Adidas. (Nike, 1960's)

➤ Become the company most known for changing the worldwide poor-quality image of Japanese products. (Sony, early 1950's)

➤ I have a dream that my four little children will one day live in a nation where they will not be judged by the color of their skin, but by the content of their character. (Martin Luther King, Jr.)

Your vision should be a *truly desired destination*—not just a bunch of pretty words. Only in that way will you be able to know when you have arrived. Is there a metric or an event that will tell you when you've achieved your vision and that you need to develop a new one?

Step Two: Mission. Many people confuse vision and mission. Vision is big-picture, long-range stuff. It is something you can "see" in your dream. Your mission statement defines your purpose and why people would buy from you. What is your offering? What is your commitment or promise to your client? What makes your approach different from everyone else's in such a way that it draws staff and clients to you? We might say that vision is internal and mission is focused on the client.

Here are some examples of company missions:

➤ Our mission is to provide the very best remodeling experience possible. The creation of value and a lifelong client will be the by-product of our dedication to excellence. (Progressive Builders, Inc.)

➤ We fulfill dreams through the experiences of motorcycling—by providing to motorcyclists and to the general public an expanding line of motorcycles, branded products, and services in selected market segments. (Harley-Davidson)

➤ The world on time. (FedEx)

➤ To solve unsolved problems innovatively. (3M)

➤ We do for families what no one should ever have to do. (Crime Site Cleanup Company)

➤ To give ordinary folk the chance to buy the same thing as rich people. (Walmart)

➤ Helping people see better, one hour at a time. (LensCrafters)

➤ To provide society with superior products and services that preserve and improve the quality of life. (Merck).

As we progress from vision and mission to defining our core values, we get closer and closer to today, to the observable, to the practical, to behaviors.

Step Three: Core Values. Each of us has deeply held beliefs about life and how life should be lived and about society and how people should treat each another. These beliefs are part of our soul. Do we always behave in accordance with these beliefs? No, but when we don't we suffer and often feel guilt or shame. Everyone who works with us brings their values. If there is a conflict between those and the company's, they are not a good fit. Shared values help ensure consistency in how people throughout the organization behave.

Jim Collins and Jerry Porras give the following tips on defining core values ("Building your Company's Vision," *Harvard Business Review,* #410X). They recommend working from individual values to the organizational values when defining perhaps five key values that will guide the company and all its actions.

➤ What core values do you personally bring to your work?

➤ What would you tell your children are the core values that you hold at work and that you hope they will hold when they become working adults?

➤ Which of your core values do you envision being as valid for you 100 years from now as they are today?

➤ Would you continue to hold these core values, even if at some point one or more of them became a competitive disadvantage?

➤ If you were to start a new organization tomorrow in a different line of work, what core values would you build into the new organization regardless of its industry?

I've found that core values are most effective when they are clearly defined and linked to behaviors. Obviously there is no way to represent every possible behavior but giving at least few examples can be very helpful in training staff and as discussion points.

Harley-Davidson has five written values that govern the company's approach to business:
1. Tell the truth.
2. Be fair.

3. Keep your promises.
4. Respect the individual.
5. Encourage intellectual curiosity.

It's easy to think we all would have the same understanding of each value, but we don't. Each of Harley-Davidson's values has a set of five guidelines or behaviors for demonstrating that value. These are the behaviors under "be fair:"

➤ Set clear and reasonable expectations.
➤ Give people a chance to succeed.
➤ Don't play favorites.
➤ Confront "head on," not "behind the back."
➤ Search for solutions where all parties benefit.

Once you've defined these values and behaviors on which the company will be built, you now have a platform for choosing and judging actions—toward the client, toward the community, and toward employees, vendors, and trade contractors. When someone tramples one of these core values, a dispassionate (much less personal) and constructive critique can be given.

Some Thoughts on Core Values

Pick up any newspaper and scan the headlines. Inevitably some of the most contentious issues relate to values, which one dictionary defines as beliefs of a person or social group in which they have an emotional investment (either for or against something).

My current newspaper has lots of fodder for this essay. While the Internet is all about free flow of information, our major search engines are being accused of permitting restrictions to be put on that flow in China. They've even been accused of helping law enforcement in China to punish those using the Internet for purposes that would be completely legitimate in other countries. The search engines acknowledge that there is a collision between the governmental culture of a huge marketplace nation like China and their company values.

Then there is the volatile issue of whether it is proper to show any likeness of a religious figure. That has caused riots around the world. Yet, for most Westerners, this is a "what's there to get excited about?" issue.

Do we belong in Iran? Or Iraq? Or Libya? If so, on what basis—weapons of mass destruction, preservation of oil, human rights? It's all a question of values. Why are politics and religion considered volatile conversations to start? Because they enter the world of values each of us hold dear but which may not match between any two of us.

Core values are often written about and talked about in business. Every business has them, but few businesses have raised them to a conscious level. They can be characterized as the rules by which the company plays the game of business.

Jim Collins, author of the books *Built to Last* and *Good to Great*, has defined core values as values you hold to be so fundamental that you would hold them regardless of whether or not they were rewarded. Typically, an entrepreneurial company assumes the values of the owner. But typically, they have to be learned by new employees by trial and error. Since they are not usually written down anywhere, the new hire learns "what we do here" and "what we don't do here" thru praise and criticism, by watching others, and by stories of incidents in the history of the company and by making mistakes.

Because this discovery process is so inefficient, an employee who isn't a good values match with a company may remain in place for a long time. This is exacerbated by a reluctance on the part of most company owners to let an employee go because of attitude or value issues.

Want to take your company to the next level? Want to create a more harmonious and unified work environment? Why not define the five top core values of your company in writing? Get your staff to help you but be sure that you, the owner, has the last word and are satisfied with the result. Define each value and add three to five types of behavior under each that you want to encourage. Then you can hire with them in hand and use them in rewarding behaviors and in disciplining behaviors.

By listing and defining the five top core values of a company in writing, you are going to help everyone in the company move toward a more perfect realization of those values. For instance, you may define "respect for the individual" as one of your company's core values. An individual whose behavior is disrespectful can now be reminded that they are out of line with that agreed-upon guide. An employee who feels that a client has been mistreated can bring that forth with greater assurance. Having written and lived core values means we know how we want to play the game in this company. They call out to us to stretch to perfect our behavior.

And for those search engine spokespeople who say that they had to abide by China's laws even though it put them on the wrong side of their company values, they might reread Jim Collins, who defines core values as values that you would want the organization to continue to hold, even if at some point they became a competitive disadvantage.

Step Four: Defining Your USP. No, this is not the United States Postal Service. It is your *unique selling proposition.* In other words, in the remodeling world of cut-throat, underselling competition, what is your uncopyable superiority? What is your exploitable advantage? What differentiates you from your competitors and gives prospects a reason to buy from you even if you are more expensive?

If you are like most remodelers, you are about to say "Great service and great craftsmanship." But stop. The problem there is that *that* is exactly what most remodelers will say. That means it is not unique to you. I wish I could tell you this will be easy. It's a little like trying to define what makes yourself unique. You will struggle, but your best friend will sum it up in a sentence. And with your USP, it's not just what makes your company unique but what will make you stand out from the competition and appeal to your prime client/prospect?

You may feel a bit silly doing this, but ask your clients why they bought from you. What was it that sold them? Try to get 10 to 15 honest answers. I think you could be surprised at what you hear. Then build that into a USP.

The website www.entrepreneur.com lists these helpful questions for defining your uniqueness—your brand:

➤ What is unique about your business or brand vs. that of your direct competitors? You'll probably find a whole list of things that set you apart; the next questions will help you decide which of these to focus on.

➤ Which of these factors is most important to the buyers and end users of your business or brand?

➤ Which of these factors is not easily imitated by competitors?

➤ Which of these factors can be easily communicated and understood by buyers or end users?

Maybe some examples of USPs will help.

➤ The nighttime, coughing, achy, sniffling, stuffy head, fever, so you can rest medicine. (Nyquil)

➤ Speed, consistency, fun for kids. (McDonald's)

➤ Fresh, hot pizza delivered to your door in 30 minutes or less. (Domino's)

➤ When your package absolutely positively has to get there overnight. (FedEx)

➤ The chocolate melts in your mouth, not in your hand. (M&M's)

➤ Builds strong bones 12 ways. (Wonder Bread)

➤ Low fares, lots of flights, lots of fun. (Southwest Airlines)

What's the point of having gone through this exercise? You'll now use consistent messaging about your uniqueness in the marketplace in every piece of literature, on your website, in your tagline, and in your sales system. You'll work to strengthen your position and create distance between you and your competitors. All your marketing will transmit this USP and because you've researched its viability in the marketplace, prospects will be attracted.

So, to Sum Up...

Section One of your business plan will list these items—

➤ Your vision

➤ Your mission

➤ Your core values

➤ Your USP

Don't feel you have to be perfect on the first go-round. Give it some time—but not too much—and get it going. You'll have years to improve and wordsmith and even change these key foundation principles. As Tom Peters says (and I do, too), "Ready, fire, aim."

Now let's move to page two of the business plan, where we will see how our business is doing now and learn a bit from our past history.

Section Two: Where are You Coming From?

I'm just finishing the book *Eat Pray Love* by Elizabeth Gilbert. In a chapter about her extended stay in Indonesia she writes, "When you are walking down the road in Bali and you pass a stranger, the very first question he or she will ask you is, 'Where are you going?' The second question is, 'Where are you coming from?'" These are not bad questions. We are going to reverse and start by asking (as we plan strategically) "Where are you coming from?" In our planning we want to put two pins on the map—the first is where we are now and the second is where we want to go. Then we can make sure that all our actions put us and keep us on the shortest path between the two.

While you are going to end up with one page, here are some backup documents and activities that will help you assess your current position in the market. Involve as many staff members as you can in doing the first two steps.

➤ Do a SWOT analysis for the company. SWOT stands for strengths, weaknesses, opportunities, and threats. The first two areas are internal; the second two are external. Use big sheets of paper and get everyone throwing out ideas. Take about 30 to 45 minutes to do this.

➤ Do a SWOT analysis for each "department" or area of the company (admin, sales, estimating, production, finance, marketing, design, etc.) Take about 20 minutes for each department. Break these first two steps into a couple of days so folks are fresh.

➤ Look big picture—assemble a 5-year financial history (a summary) showing your volume, gross profit dollars and percentage, overhead dollars and net profit percentage and dollars. Examine the trends. Did overhead outgrow volume growth? Are you consistently profitable? Is your job-cost percentage showing creep? Are your clients highly satisfied? What is working and what isn't?

➤ Go departmental—write a review of your last 3 to 5 years of performance that presents a *concise* assessment of your current position in every "department." Are you woefully understaffed? Do you need a uniform method of estimating? Will sales training improve your volume? Is your marketing old fashioned and out-of-date or do you need consistent messaging? Does your website stand out in representing who you are? Does it rank well in search engine optimization?

So, to Sum Up...

Now take what you've discovered and boil it down to one page. Focus on the strengths that you want to maximize and the weaknesses that you want to minimize in the future.

Section Two of your business plan will include:

1. Your assessment of the company operation as a whole over the last 3 (or 4, or 5) years.

2. Three major changes that would drastically improve the company's overall success and one or more metrics on each that would measure your progress toward that success.

3. Two to three changes in each department that would make major improvements in that department's success—with metrics.

Section Three: Where are You Going?

Now for the fun, look-into-the-future part. We get to dream, vision, and plan where we want to be within a time frame. It's exciting and full of possibilities. By writing it down, you will really contemplate how possible it will be and what tradeoffs you will need to make to achieve your plan. Here are five steps:

1. Pick your *time frame.* In these turbulent times, I would suggest that you use a 3- to 5-year time frame. That's also a very accessible time frame, especially if you are just starting to plan. Most of us feel pretty confident looking out that distance. But if you want to sell the company in 8 years or if there is a particularly important deadline, go ahead and choose that.

2. Write a concise *"picture"* of what the company looks like at the end of that time frame. Include volume, net profit, and your salary. What roles will need to be filled—what new job descriptions? Very importantly, what role will you be filling? Will the company be large enough that you won't be involved in the day-to-day operations? Or will you put down your production hat and only do sales? How about your physical plant? Will you be operating from your home, a new office, a bigger office, a

showroom, or multiple locations? Flesh this concise picture out so that it is not dispassionate but has a really tangible "feel" to it.

3. List five key *Strategic priorities* that you want to achieve in this time frame along with how you would measure attainment (metrics). Because this is a longer range plan, restricting the number will force you to choose wisely. It's likely that these will tie back into the changes you listed on page two of your plan.

   An example might be that you will double the percentage of your volume that is design/build from 43% to 85%. Or that you will pay off all debt and build a $20,000 "rainy day fund." Or that you will develop a comprehensive training program for field personnel. At this point, we are not listing how we intend to execute on that strategy. We will do that in the annual plan.

4. Create the *organizational chart* of your company at the end of the time frame. Highlight any new roles you will need at that time to operate the company you envision. For example, you might be planning to add one administrative clerk, one designer, one salesperson, and one junior production manager as well as three field crews. Add the year you plan to bring the new hire on board.

5. Create a *budget summary* for the end point (and even budgets for every year if you like). For example, maybe you plan to be a $4.2 million company with a markup of 50%, a gross profit of 31% (allowing for 2% slippage), and a net profit of 8%. Dive deeper and sketch out your overhead requirements given what you want to achieve. Be sure to take inflation into account. You'll want to be sure that changes to the organizational chart are included. Will there be new office or showroom changes? Do you need to allow for a commissioned sales force? Will this new bigger company require a higher markup?

Now boil all this down to one page—the third Section of your business plan. As with all these pages, you may have backup material (for instance, a fully drawn out organizational plan for each year, but you would summarize for page three).

➤ Check *alignment*. From Section One to Section Three of your business plan, all should feel cohesive and aligned. Your strategies should be attainable within the framework of your mission and vision. They should be in harmony with the "picture" of the company you want to have at the end of the time frame. You should be comfortable that the plan is optimistically realistic.

Do you think this would be a stimulating and motivating document for you and your personnel? Would it help fire you up? Would it help harness all your staff to pull in the same direction? I think it would, or I wouldn't be suggesting that you do it.

Each year go back, make adjustments, and be sure it is a living document that responds to changing conditions. Good luck!

Zoom In on Your 1-Year Plan

Now that you have the longer term strategic business plan in place, it's time to decide just how much distance you can attain toward your goals in the next year. This annual plan will focus on the financial, the organizational, the marketing, and three to five major measurable objectives for the company supported by three to five measurable objectives for each "department" in your company. It will be much more detailed. It will be the first big step from where you are today moving toward where you want to be in 3-5 years. Let's talk about each of these areas.

1. *Financial* (one to two pages): Develop a budget (or budgets) for the year. Use the categories from your P&L reports and project how much volume you can sell, at what gross profit, with what overhead and what resulting net.

   Please be realistic here. If you overestimate volume or gross profit, your plan is doomed. That's why you might want to develop a number of scenarios and pick the most likely one. You will be adjusting your budget regularly anyway as factors change. Go for a net profit of 5 to 8% (in downtimes) and 10% or more in good times.

   After budgeting the entire year to your satisfaction, break it down into a 12-month spreadsheet. Don't just divide by 12 but try to put actual expenditures into the months they will be expended.

2. *Organizational* (one to two pages): Are you happy with your current organization, the people, the roles, and the handoffs? If so, there's no need to worry about this one. But typically, companies plan to grow and may need to add staff or shift some tasks or roles around. Be sure you are developing the "A" team and don't keep marginal players. Draw out your organizational chart. Note where a position is a new one.

3. *Marketing plan, budget, and calendar* (two to three pages). There's lots more about this piece in the Marketing section, but you want to start your year knowing how many leads you will need given your close ratio and how you will generate those leads.

   Accompanying the plan for what outreach tactics you will use should be a ballpark budget for each item and a calendar showing when tasks need to be done. This calendar will also let you see when expenditures will be needed. Many companies develop vague plans with no budget or calendar. By developing a specific plan and adding the budget and calendar and who is charged to implement the plan, you are much more likely to have a successful marketing outreach.

4. *Define three to six major measurable company objectives* (two to three pages, including #5 below). Make sure these are important objectives and that you list how they will be measured and who is responsible for them. They are likely to be "way stations" on the road to accomplishing the goals in your long term plan.

   Here are some examples:

   ➤ To penetrate the Knollwood Hills subdivision as measured by getting at least three jobs over $20,000 in size there.

   ➤ To increase our gross profit by 8% through increased markup (+2%), better estimating (+2%), job handoff (+1%), and job performance (+3%) as measured by our P&L.

   ➤ To open a window-replacement division headed by Jim Koch and sell and produce at least $400,000 this first year.

   ➤ To increase our client satisfaction rate from 85% to 90% as measured by our third party evaluation firm.

5. *Measurable departmental objectives.* Your SWOT analysis of each department undoubtedly uncovered some weaknesses and opportunities. In addition, the company objectives above impact a variety of departments. Set three to five objectives for each department that support the business plan strategies and objectives and that also support the objectives for the next year.

6. *Spell out action steps* (one to ? pages). What specific actions will be taken to achieve the company and departmental objectives, by whom, and by when? This will allow you to be sure you aren't "biting off more than you can chew" and that no one person has too much to handle. You may have to do some changing and some shuffling before you settle on the highest priority action steps.

For instance, in the second objective above, if we are focusing on the estimating function, then we will need some action steps related to making our estimates more accurate (we may need new software, we may need firm subcontractor bids, subcontractors may need to visit the site before giving a number, or we may need to add to our estimates in some historically weak areas, etc.) Achieving that second objective of increasing gross profit will impact sales, estimating, possibly design, the handoff package, and procedure from sales to production and production training, monitoring, etc. Everyone will have their part to play.

Again, check the *alignment* within the 1-year plan and with your longer term business plan. Are you taking real strides to accomplish what you said you wanted to accomplish? Because measurements are spelled out, you and your key managers will be able to assess how you are doing and make course corrections along the way. You'll want to meet monthly to check on how everyone's contribution is going and whether you are moving along as expected.

In our company we start this process in November with the entire team. By the end of December we have the plan agreed upon and in place by the end of December.

Again I ask, do you think that if you and your team took this time and effort to plan the year that your results could be improved? Would you be moving to a better and better company each year? Would your personnel be united in achieving the same goals that you want? I say "Yes!" to all three of those questions. I hope you do, too.

Marking Up

Your ability to carry out your strategic business plan is related to your ability to sell profitable jobs effectively. In addition, a recessionary economy (in place as I write) makes markup and pricing the issue of the hour. We are getting many inquiries about whether this tight market calls for a tighter price. This is a controversial subject and no matter what I write, there will be those who disagree. Let's review how to plan your need for markup and then let's review some different ways to mark up.

Figure Out an Appropriate Markup

A decision on markup begins with knowing exactly how much you will spend on overhead plus how much you want in net profit. In better times, I pushed companies to aim for an 8 to 10% net (over and above the owner's salary), and that allows for some erosion from cost overruns because they are so frequent. These days, I'm looking for a 5 to 8% net when our clients plan their year but I will loudly applaud any additional net they feel they can earn.

So if you know your overhead cost (including your salary) plus your desired net profit, you know the required gross profit that your markup must provide. Say you realistically anticipate $1.2 million in volume, your overhead is going to be $324,000 (27%), and you are planning for a 6% net (72,000). Thus, you need 33% gross profit or $396,000. Let's convert that gross profit into the markup you will need by subtracting your gross profit percentage from 1 and then dividing 1 by the answer ($1 - 0.33 = 0.67$; 1 divided by 0.67 = 1.49). In this case, the direct costs will be $804,000 x 1.49 = $1.2 million.

Gross Profit Benchmarks for Professional Remodelers.

Remember, these are benchmarks—an amalgam of what other companies need. You may need more or less gross profit for your company, but it pays to be clear why you need more or less. The overhead portion of gross profit is clearly tied to average job size. The larger the average job size, the lower the overhead per volume dollar.

The smaller the average job size, the higher the overhead per volume dollar. So overhead could range from 12% in the extremely-big-job-size group to 30 to 40% for a company with much smaller job sizes, a showroom, a strong marketing program, and, perhaps, commissioned sales. However, goals for the net profit portion of gross profit would be similar no matter the average job size. Today's remodelers have cut overhead substantially and even leaned down the net in many cases so that markups overall are leaner.

But no matter how lean the professional remodeler gets, there are many competitors in your marketplace that will undercut you substantially because they don't know their costs and overhead. As Chad Vincent, owner of Renaissance Remodeling in Boise, Idaho, reminds us, "What makes any of us believe that it is the $5,000 less that makes them (prospects) buy from us? If we compete with other companies, rarely is there a great choice of two or three companies within $5,000 with all the same qualities. "

Many Roads to Marking Up

It doesn't matter how you mark up as long as you bring home the bacon. To mix metaphors, you can charge the homeowners your cost on the job and sell cupcakes at the end of the driveway. But if you are the aforementioned $1.2 million remodeler, you must end up with $396,000 at the end of the year to pay your overhead and show a net for your efforts and your risk.

Now let's look at some different ways a job can be marked up.

Gross profit per hour based on carpentry hours. If you take your field personnel for the year (say six, for example) and multiply by 1700 hours or so, figuring that is their *actual* working time, you will get the number of man/person hours that has to provide the GP that you need for your overhead and your net.

Divide GP dollars needed by those hours and you will get the GP per hour. You can then use that to price jobs (using the burdened averaged hourly cost of a field person and adding GP per hour). This works only if you perform carpentry with employed carpenters rather than trade contractors.

If you move from an across-the-board markup to a gross profit per hour markup, this will make the jobs that are light on carpentry less expensive than now and heavy-on-carpentry jobs more expensive than now. Potentially, it will swing the mix of your jobs to the former. You are betting that you can utilize all the required hours on the jobs you actually do.

This takes some sophisticated financial skills since you aren't aiming for that volume you planned for in your budget. Your volume may be higher or lower. It can be dangerous but then everything we do can be dangerous!

Gross profit per week. This works whether you have your own crews or not. Divide the annual needed GP by 52 (or 51, if you don't work the holiday week). As you price jobs, *assuming you are accurate on scheduling* (a big assumption in this business), look at how much GP they will produce by the week. That will tell you if you should/could raise or lower prices. One remodeler I know did this and decided he couldn't make money doing bathrooms. It will give you a different perspective. It will also put an emphasis on accurate scheduling in your company—and that's a good thing.

The Bottom Line

There's a reason why the most popular markup system is an across-the-board one. It's easy, doesn't let you rationalize to lower prices, and doesn't require the financial sophistication of the other systems. Personally, I'd recommend that you price at least two ways and use your best judgment on what fits the job you are looking at while watching your P&L and Work in Progress reports (WIP) like a hawk.

Joanne Hall, co-owner of Villa Builders, Inc., in Arnold, Md., advises, "it's like sailing—you have to trim, jibe, tack, reef the main, and sometimes just turn the damn engine on. I don't think you can ever, or should ever believe you can just set your sail and forget it....not anymore."

Want a Shorter Planning Process?

There are two business planning tools I wouldn't consider entering a new year without. They are important every year you are in business. The first is the budget or plan for how you will make profit. The second is your marketing plan that shows exactly how you will attract the right kind of leads that will generate the right kind of sales in your company.

With the economy in an uproar, budgeting aggressively has <u>never</u> been more important than now. Our most successful clients live their budget. Many have told us that the knowledge that their budget provided was a crucial tool used to help them stay in business and healthy during the last twelve months. It will be even more important in the next year.

So if in the past you've ignored the budgeting process because you felt you didn't have any control over the economy, **reverse course now!** There is much you do control and you must have a roadmap to negotiate these treacherous business waters.

Here are four guidelines to help:

Plan realistically.
This probably is a year to hunker down and get back to basics. There are three numbers you need to hit correctly—volume, gross profit percentage, and overhead percentage. If you overstate either of the first two or underestimate the third, your plan will be in trouble.

Share risk.
Get buy-in. Bring your staff into the inner circle and get them to help you scrutinize every line item in overhead and job costs. Pick their best money-saving or marketing ideas and assign a champion to drive it and metrics to measure success on a regular basis. Your leadership has never been more important.

Update monthly.
Every month, meet with your staff to review your actual numbers against your budget, forecast the remaining portion of the year so that you recognize where the company stands, and then develop an action plan to immediately get your plan back into balance.

Have a backup plan ready in your desk drawer. What if your budget was too rosy? Know exactly **what you'll do** and **when you'll do it** to bring your company back to profitability. Having this plan prepared in advance will enable you to be nimble and make fast, effective changes.

If you and your staff don't feel that you have the knowledge or expertise to create the plan you need, reach out to those who do. Whether it's your accountant or a business consultant, this is a critical key to your company's survival and ability to thrive!

Let's talk marketing. As with your budget, you can create a long, complex, 100-page plan or a short concise one. I vote for the latter. Here are some guidelines:

Do the math.

How many leads do you need? You can get this number by figuring how many first appointments it takes for you to sell one job. Then look at how many incoming inquiries it takes for you to generate those first appointments. In good times, it often takes eight incoming calls to generate five first appointments to generate one sale. If your average sale is $25,000 and you need $1 million in sales this year, you are ready to do the math. You need 40 jobs and 320 leads. Be aware that many companies today have seen a doubling of the number of incoming calls it takes to generate one sale.

Define the demographics of the client who buys your job.

Look at your past history and your client database. Can you narrow down to a solid household income range, to the right neighborhoods, to the jobs where your company makes the most money and does the best job? This information will be invaluable in honing your marketing to the clients you want. It will let you prioritize your selling efforts.

Focus most of your marketing effort on two areas.

Those areas are your circle of influence (past client base and friends of the company) and on tactics that get you face-to-face contact with prospects (seminars, networking groups, local charitable foundations, etc.) Be sure you are marketing-focused with these two groups and invite (and thank people for) referral leads.

Diversify your marketing dollars.

In today's market, I would budget at least 3 to 5% of your volume for marketing if you are a full-line remodeler. This money should be spread between many activities so that if any one is a bust, the others will help support your lead flow.

Hopefully, you've been doing these two plans over the past years so you have honed your ability to predict outcomes. If not, get started now. Don't leave home without them!

chapter six

MAGNETIC MARKETING

What, No Plan? Here's How

Ten Marketing Tactics That Work

Guerrilla Tactics:
What's Working in Marketing

Simplicity Wins

You've Got Homework!

Gathering Intelligence Revisited

> *"If you don't believe in your product, or if you're not consistent and regular in the way you promote it, the odds of succeeding go way down. The primary function of the* **marketing plan** *is to ensure that you have the resources and the wherewithal to do what it takes to make your product work."*
>
> Jay Levinson

The history of remodeling is fairly devoid of marketing. The typical remodeler started with the first job and then relied on word of mouth to spread the news of their good work and bring in the next job. Only the biggest full-line remodelers spent 1 to 2% of their volume on marketing and they were self taught. Specialty remodelers, such as window, door, and deck companies, spent more like 8 to 10% to market and were much more marketing savvy. It was a mark of pride that full-line remodelers would say that they didn't need marketing—all their leads were referrals. As I write, the economic realities have put this era behind us.

What are the changes?

Over the past few years every remodeler has had to up their marketing game—and expenditures—to survive. It's now common for the full-line remodeler to spend 4 to 5% of their projected volume in marketing outreaches while the single-line specialty remodeler will spend 10 to 15%.

In addition, many of the outreaches and tactics that used to work no longer do. You used to be able to spend money on postcards, ads, and printed newsletters to create a predictable flow of leads. Now, lead flow is directly related to who you know, how many folks you are interacting with, and how many organizations you are active in. So not only has the expense gone up, the time involvement has as well. Marketing today must be a major priority in every company.

To be successful, today's marketing programs must be very diversified. It's not uncommon to have 20 to 30 lead sources. Each area of marketing brings in fewer leads than it used to, but, by having many "fishing lines in the water," each bringing in a modest amount of leads, you find the number of prospects you need to sell your volume.

Marketing has become more complex. Website sophistication has escalated and your website is a living brochure that must be kept up to date and optimized for search engines. Social media have become important and will likely continue to be an ever more important tool in the marketing toolbox. This is both good and bad news. You can attract prospects who are searching online or who know about you and are trying to find you. But the bad news is that clients can now bash your company in online reviews and you need to track and reply to any of these comments. Negative reviews can be devastating to your business.

Because marketing has become more complex and is of the highest priority, company owners have increasingly brought in some outside expertise to help plan, budget, and implement their marketing.

What, No Plan? Here's How

You and I meet at a business mixer in your hometown and start talking—what else?—business. You learn I have a dog boarding kennel and that I am trying to grow both my volume of business as well as my bottom line net profit. You start asking me a barrage of questions on how I will fuel that growth. Where will the new business come from? What kind of business is most profitable for me? How much will I spend to attract that new business? And how will I spend it? In other words, do I have a plan and a budget to fund my growth? My answers are vague and unfocused. You are disappointed to learn that while I have a lot of hope, I really have no plan. Mentally, you question my business acumen and you move on to talk to a local lawyer.

It's often easier to diagnose what's needed in someone else's company. But now let's turn those logical questions around to your business. I've found many remodelers are amazingly lackadaisical about marketing. They take an "If I dream it, it will come" approach to assuring business growth or even business viability. Quality leads are what feeds everyone in your company. It is a huge risk not to manage the intake pipe for work. At the same time, developing a good marketing plan and funding and implementing that plan is not rocket science. We know what it takes and that's following these seven steps.

Set the goals for your marketing outreach.

The obvious answer here is "leads," but the real answer is "too many leads of the right quality." Having too many leads means you can pick and choose—geographically, by job type, and by job size. It means you can charge a higher markup, have more prospects drop off, and still have the right number of jobs. So even if you have enough leads to reach your business goals, you may well have other needs that mean a constant marketing presence.

Create your marketing plan.

Think *strategies* and *tactics* here. Strategies are the major objectives you want to accomplish with your marketing. Here are some examples of strategies:

➤ We want to move from an architect-bid company to design/build.

➤ We want to penetrate the Knollwood subdivision market.

➤ We want to move from $25,000 average job size to $35,000.

➤ We want to become known as the "go-to" company in the seismic retrofit market.

➤ We want to add a landscape design/build division.

As you can see, these are major objectives but none of these statements say exactly how we plan to do this with our marketing. What activities will we do? Those outreaches are tactics. So under every strategy would be a list of actual marketing outreaches that will work to achieve those big objectives.

Start with your strategies/objectives. What do you want your marketing to do for your company? Think of marketing as a driver that will help you go in the direction you desire. You could bring in a marketing expert to help you with this but, in the final analysis, always trust your brain and gut. Marketing plans should be approved at the owner level but implemented by someone else in the company or outsourced. As you can see, deciding the strategies that your marketing plan addresses is high level work.

Focus your tactics.
Your starting points should be a careful review of what worked and what did not in the previous year, plus a round of brainstorming on ways to market the company. Make sure your tactics fit your strategies and your budget but plan out the entire year. Marketing outreaches often take 6 months to yield results.

Fund your marketing.
Most remodelers seem to spend about 1% of their volume for marketing, but then most remodelers are poor marketers. Plan instead to spend 3 to 5% of your projected volume if you are a full-line remodeler. If you have a showroom, add 5%. If you sell jobs that average $10,000 or less, you may well need 10 to 12% of your projected volume to achieve the right number of leads. While these amounts may sound like a lot—especially if you've been spending almost nothing—remember that their purpose is to assure enough work of the right type for the company. Think of it as very important insurance that your company will stay in business.

Schedule your marketing.
Once you know your tactics and budget, it's time to put your activities on a

calendar. Maybe you'll send an e-newsletter quarterly. Don't stop there. That newsletter needs to be written, photos may need to be taken, etc. Each of those activities should also go on the calendar. Now you can be sure of two things: Is your marketing consistent year-round? Can you afford the expenditures as they are shown?

Implement your marketing.

Once the plan, budget, and calendar are in place, the implementation of marketing is relatively easy. You could assign it to your office manager, your designer, or whoever has an interest in running it. Many companies outsource it to a freelancer who meets with the owner at least monthly. They should report to you to review the results to date and what is planned for the following month so you can change course if you need to.

Track your marketing.

Track results carefully. Remodelers who have managed the first six steps often falter on this last critical one. To make good marketing decisions you need careful detailing of the source of every incoming raw (before qualification) lead, whether you trashed it, whether it turned into a first appointment, whether it turned into a design contract, whether that prospect purchased construction, and the sale price of the resulting job. You will then be able to see the cost of each lead by marketing source, the cost of each sale by source, and the average size of the jobs by source. There will be no mystery in what is working for you and what is not.

These seven steps will give you control of your lead flow. You'll know how to increase leads when you want to and this knowledge will help you thrive through the years. It's a must-do.

Ten Marketing Tactics That Work

Every smart remodeler is covered by insurance against catastrophe. But there is one type of coverage many lack. That's the coverage that assures that the intake pipeline for work stays full. Many, many remodelers give marketing—the insurance that fills that pipeline—short shrift.

We've explored planning and tracking your marketing. Today, I want to cover the top 10 marketing outreaches that work. They aren't the most sophisticated but they work, year after year. I'll start at the bottom, Letterman-style.

10. Developing an e-mail database and sending to it six times during the year. A small company should have 200 to 300 names, addresses, and e-mail addresses in its database, so be sure to capture e-mails of all prospects, all clients, and all friends of the company who are likely to refer to you. Since e-mail is so inexpensive, you don't have to cull your e-mail the way you used to when you were using your database to "snail" mail.

9. Association membership. I wouldn't have thought of this until I heard Steve Dormann of S & D Renovations Inc., a $2.5 million remodeler in Emmaus, Pa., recently tell how his remodeling association membership has brought him 12% of his volume. He listed links to the website, awards, referrals, and more. He obviously uses every opportunity to mine his membership for marketing angles.

8. Home tours. Often, tours are the result of an association's efforts and they are soft sell and very effective. One remodeler, who had three projects in the same neighborhood, ran his own tour. If you use this tactic, don't forget security, dust protection, food, and more.

7. Publicity. When you talk about your company, it's advertising. When your newspaper or your radio or your TV talks about you, it's powerful third-party testimonial. It's often inexpensive to engage a local freelance public relations professional to design and implement six stories about you, your company, or your projects over the next year. Don't forget entering projects for awards and then publicizing the wins.

6. High community profile. Here's a chance to take what you enjoy—golf, sailing, biking, charitable outreach—and turn it to your company's advantage. Don't be bashful and don't be brash, but let folks know what you do. They'll put that together with the fact they like and admire you and will call you for their next remodeling project. Also consider seminars for the public here. Take every opportunity to meet and greet and to position yourself as "the remodeling expert."

5. Jobsite presence. Do you have a distinctive sign that shows your craftsmanship and is readable from the street? You might want to include a brochure box—like real estate pros do—on the post. You could also do one, two, or three letters to the 50 to 100 neighbors near the jobsite. After all, you have a "showroom" in their neighborhood. You also have a built-in testimonial.

4. Your website. This used to be an option, but no more. Yes, it is a new kind of brochure for your company with great photos, but it should be informative, should stress your uniqueness when compared with your competition, and should encourage new prospects to contact you.

3. A great image. This becomes particularly important for design/build companies. It starts with a logo and a look—colors and fonts. This includes your signage, your stationary, and your website. It should all be consistent and great looking. Don't skimp here.

2. Sterling customer service. No remodeler can afford to constantly market for new clients. By pleasing your current buyers, you create friends of the company. Because happy clients tell 3 to 5 of their friends and unhappy ones tell 10 or more (unless they give you a scathing review online, in which case thousands), you are playing an important mathematical game of keeping good words out on the street about your company. Consider everything you do to delight your buyers as part of your marketing.

and, drum roll, please...

1. Past customers and friends of the company program. This is the always-was-and-always-will-be number one marketing outreach. Staying in touch with your past clients and referrers four to six times a year keeps their loyalty strong and keeps them referring you year after year. Vary your contacts from newsletters to invitations to special events. And don't forget a written thank-you for every referral. Companies have summer picnics, get-togethers, and special perks like Christmas tree cuttings for this expanded sales force.

It's a tremendous responsibility to run a business on which your family and your employees, your trade contractors and vendors and their families depend. Don't forget that intake pipeline insurance—your marketing!

Guerrilla Tactics: What's Working in Marketing

Times for most remodelers are hard. There are fewer buyers and less urgent buyers. Job sizes are smaller. But you can't even begin to sell until you have a lead. And leads are fewer and less qualified. Many of the marketing techniques that traditionally have worked are not working now. So what is?

Interestingly, it's a form of marketing that takes less money but more time. Networking. I'm hearing over and over that there is work out there but you have to get out of the office to get it—and it comes from a million different places and from people who have learned about you in some way—often unrelated to your business.

Listen to Ken Kirsch, co-owner of MAK Design + build in Davis, Calif. "I have attended events at the Davis Downtown Business Association, the Chamber of Commerce, NARI, and a city-sponsored green-building event," says the busy remodeler, who enjoys painting as a hobby. "I have also placed paintings in a new building that a Realtor friend is selling. A kitchen job in which we got the go-ahead earlier this week is a lead from that Realtor. One lead this week came from the NARI directory, which the prospective client picked up at the NARI booth at a home show in January."

MAK also got a job from a homeowner who met Kirsch at an elementary school fair, where he was face-painting while wearing a hat printed with the company's logo. "The client told me that he thought that anybody who gave that much attention to the detail in painting a child's face must also be a meticulous builder," says the remodeler. Jeff King of Jeff King and Company, Inc., in San Francisco has had a number of jobs result from his association with fellow parents at his children's private school.

Allison Guido of Almar Building and Remodeling Co., Inc., in Hanover, Mass., has committed to a planned networking program that in 1 month alone includes a Business Expo (300 attendees in 8 hours), participating in an Asthma Walk where Almar is the leading corporate fundraiser and employees will wear logoed T-shirts, hosting a workshop on effective networking in their offices, and presenting an Aging in Place adult education class at three locations.

While we all think we know how to network, there is actually some science behind doing it well. Here are some tips:

Today's effective networking isn't lackadaisical. It is a planned and funded part of the company's marketing outreach. The organizations you'll join or participate in are carefully chosen to fit your interests but also to have the right demographics for your client base. Are the organization's members people who would make good clients for you or who know people who would make good clients?

Be prepared with your "elevator" speech. How would you explain what your company does in the short time between the 1st and 10th floors? That's only time for a few sentences which should communicate clearly. And they should communicate how you are different from your competitors. Be sure you have business cards and brochures to hand out—but only when appropriate.

Be prepared to refer others. Right now, I'm trying to find a good painter and a good roofer and I am asking those I trust for referrals. Huge amounts of business are awarded that way. This will be a give-and-take proposition.

Engage everyone on your staff. They are out in their groups, too—PTA, churches, Habitat for Humanity, and more. Role-play good networking behaviors. Make sure they carry cards. Be willing to pay for their membership to additional groups they would be interested in joining. Consider a reward for every lead brought into the office and a bigger reward for those that result in a sale.

Don't forget to thank the referrer. A hand-written note, a golf outing with you, a lunch or dinner, or tickets to a ball game with you will all express your appreciation and encourage repeat referrals.

While the out-of-pocket costs of networking outreaches tend to be relatively small, the time commitment is large—and that still comes down to money. So be sure to keep statistics on how leads come to you so you know what to repeat and what to drop.

Yes, times are tougher. The game is changing and we have to change, too. But once you master networking, I don't think you'll ever go back.

Simplicity Wins

I am a nut about feedback. If I've learned one thing in my business and consulting life, it is to ask every client how I am doing. This has to go hand in hand with making them feel comfortable about being honest. My business has profited enormously from being guided by what works for our clients but even more by learning what doesn't work.

However, my downfall has always been wanting to ask every possible question and gather every nugget from a client survey. You have their valuable attention for a moment, so how can you squeeze the maximum from that interaction? On the other hand, I've always wanted, and advised others, to include some way to compile their surveys into one number that can be compared quarter to quarter, year to year.

No more. I've seen the light. I've just learned that there is a survey question that will tell me who will enthusiastically refer more business to me, will buy again from me, and will foretell my company's future for growth and industry domination. Plus, I've learned a simple new process for obtaining a final number that can be compared year to year. Interested?

It's called the **Net-Promoter Score**. The question is "How likely is it that you would recommend (the company) to a friend or colleague?" The answer is picked from a scale of 1 to 10, where 10 means "extremely likely," 5 means "neutral," and 0 means "not at all likely."

Nothing is too new and different about that. But the process of scoring the survey answers is quite different.

Answers are tallied in only two categories. The highly positive answers—9s and 10s—are compiled and the percentage they represent of the total survey is figured. These enthusiastic referrers are considered the *promoters* of the company. Then those who answered with a lackluster 0 to 6 are tallied and the percentage they represent of the total is figured. These folks are designated as *detractors*.

The result subtracts the detractor percentage (say 20%) from the promoter percentage (say 49%) to get a net-promoter score (in the example, 29%).

This isn't hard and it makes sense. In remodeling, we've long known the high value of referrers to our businesses. But this process creates a metric that has statistical validity and by which we can monitor our progress or lack of progress from year to year.

The one-question focus does not mean that you cannot mine more detail from your clients. You may well want to do phone or in-person follow-up interviews with some who gave you very high scores and some who gave you marginal or low scores. That will give you more detailed data with which to accentuate the positive and eliminate the negative.

The study's author, Frederick Reichheld, notes, "The median net-promoter score of more than 400 companies in 28 industries...was just 16%.... The companies with the most enthusiastic customer referrals, including eBay, Amazon, and USAA, receive net-promoter scores of 75% to more than 80%."

There is considerable research with a capital "R" behind why this question correlates so effectively with growth and domination in an industry where other commonly asked questions do not. This fascinating study of 130,000 buyers in many industries is outlined in an article entitled "The One Number You Need to Grow," by Frederick Reichheld in *The Harvard Business Review* (12/03).

I'm off to simplify our surveys...how about you?

You've Got Homework!

How good are you as a researcher of vital intelligence for your company? What do you read? To whom do you talk? How do you keep your finger on the pulse of the local economy? It has never been more important to constantly feed on critical bits of info to update your mental database. And it's never been more important to apply this information gathering to your marketing.

We all know the marketing landscape has changed dramatically. It used to be a verdant meadow and it's now a desert populated by widely spaced cactus.

We know something else—what used to work in many cases just doesn't work any more. Many tactics, such as direct mail and newspaper and magazine advertising, often just don't justify the expense today. The bright spots in marketing involve belly-to-belly contact—or, to put it more politely, face-to-face relationship building. In general, the tactics that work today take time and not much money. The tactics that have lost their luster took money but not much time.

Here's the latest assignment I gave to two marketing classes I am teaching. Although each remodeler was not able to do each assignment, they unearthed some gold nuggets to help them shape a more effective marketing plan. Try them. They might lead your marketing in a better, more relationship-driven direction.

We're all sure we know why people buy from us but we rarely check by talking directly to them. This is different from finding out that once they worked with us, they were raving fans. Let's explore the intake side of the curve. Call five clients who represent your prime client (because of their finances, lifestyle, neighborhood, demographics, or whatever).

Try to take down verbatim and in writing what they say about how they first learned about your company, how many other contractors they interviewed, and, ultimately, why they bought from you. Focus on the marketing and selling process, not how they felt about you after the job was over. You're trying to take verbatim notes because only by doing that will you be able to assemble the group of interviews and re-read them for patterns and similar emotions. Then you can form your marketing outreach and your messages around what they tell you.

Next, make a list of all organizations to which you and your staff belong. Assess how active you are in each. Take 15 minutes and brainstorm whether there are other memberships that would help the company expand its referral network. Brainstorm with your staff how you can raise your visibility in these organizations without being obnoxious.

Let's explore "feeders" (folks, like real estate agents or interior designers, who may know of prospects before you do and could refer a stream of them to you over time) and "strategic alliances" (allied businesses like landscapers or cabinet showrooms that don't do structural changes). Yes, their business is slow, too, but that means you need more of these good people.

Hopefully, you'll be able to cross-refer prospects back to them. So make a list of complementary businesses and/or individuals with whom you are now allied. What have you done to market to them, to stay in touch, to thank them? If you haven't talked or had coffee or golfed with them in the last month, get them on your calendar. Brainstorm a list of complementary businesses and/or individuals that don't now refer to you but whom you should contact ASAP.

And lastly, do what all big companies do and almost no remodelers do—gather intelligence on your competitors. Check them out on Google, see if they have websites, and learn as much as you can about their offerings, their style, and their messages. Adventurous? Get someone (a relative, or a friend) to call three to five of your main competitors, pretending to be a prospect.

Get information from them on how they work, find out if they charge for design, ask them to send a brochure, ask them for testimonials, and write up an analysis. Could you get this person to have the competitor come to their home and do a proposal and estimate? For some remodelers, this may not feel ethical. From my perspective, gathering intelligence is critical to keeping up with what the competition is doing.

None of this costs money, but the information you will unearth is invaluable. Just don't let Fido eat *this* homework!

Gathering Intelligence Revisited

My previous suggestion about gathering valuable information from competitors raised one reader's ire. I suggested having a friend or family member call your main competitors and gather as much intelligence as possible about how they handle the call and how they handle prospects.

But I really stepped over his boundaries when I suggested that the "mystery shopper" could have the competitor come to their home and do an estimate and proposal. I suggested that going that far might not feel ethical to every company owner. And boy, was I right.

Anthony Slabaugh of Anthony M. Slabaugh Construction, Inc., in Stow, Ohio, took the time to write a well-considered letter which said, in part, "If someone called me (and maybe they have) with the intent to get information to help another remodeling contractor, and I found out, I would be furious!

It's hard enough as an owner of a remodeling business to manage time appropriately because of the amount of hats that are worn, so the idea of someone calling to purposely deceive me and waste my time is appalling. Not to mention that every phone call in this economy is treated as *gold*. So to build someone's hope up and lead them on like this is just plain cruel."

All medium and big companies do this type of research. Most small companies like us do not. There are whole firms that provide mystery shoppers who experience what the competitors have to offer and write extensive reports. Companies also purposely have their own operations shopped to find out how leads and inquiries are handled. It would not surprise or anger me if our company has been shopped.

That said, however, I have heard from other remodelers in the past about their concern at taking a competitor's time by doing this research. I am adamant that we must do research on our competitors. Only by doing that can we analyze the difference our company brings to the marketplace and how we need to sell against those companies in our markets. However, there are many different things that can be done and hopefully somewhere in the mix are some tactics that will work for you and for Anthony.

Here are seven.

1. Google "remodeling" and the town your competitors and you are in and see where your website and theirs falls in the pack. Play with other common word searches to compare. If your website doesn't come up first, learn how to get to first place whether by using blogs, links, or hidden words or purchasing ad-words. You can go to www.websitegrader.com to have it grade your website and also compare it to a competitor's. The free report will provide you with lots of suggestions on how to raise your ranking.

2. While you are looking at websites, review a competitor's website thoroughly to see how it stacks up against yours. Try to discern the major messages they are sending to prospects. How user-friendly and easy to navigate is it? What are they saying their main attributes, skills, core competencies as a company are? And while you are there at your computer, check out your website as a prospect and put it through the same paces to see how it does for you. You may be in for some surprises. How unique are your messages in the marketplace? How user-friendly is your website?

3. When you are in the hiring mode and an applicant lists a competitor as a previous workplace, don't miss the opportunity to learn a bit about the organization and its systems.

4. If you ultimately hire that applicant, you can learn more over time about the quality of the competitor's systems, training, culture, and other details without being too prying.

5. Sometimes your prospects have talked with both you and your competitor. If you get the job, ask if they would mind discussing the process with you (after the job is over) and ask about why they bought from you and why they didn't buy from any other remodelers they spoke with.

6. If you do competitive bidding, make an upfront agreement with the homeowner or the architect that you will want to know how the bids stack up pricewise once the job is granted. Don't be afraid to take architects to lunch and ask how they would characterize the various remodelers they work with. After these meetings, write down your notes and file.

7. And—I still say this—have someone call your competitor to inquire and ask for brochure, ask some simple questions (are you able to both design and then construct—do you do both? Do you charge for the design?) This tactic could also be used to shop competitors at a home show.

With all these tactics, you'll want to keep written notes in a file. Sometimes, you'll hit a dead end. But each nugget you learn is extremely valuable to your company. I would be the last person to ask you to step over your values line. Just remember that each of us have slightly differing values that support our integrity. Stay with what makes you comfortable.

chapter seven

WHEN BUSINESS GIVES YOU LEMONS

The Mock Burial That Didn't Work

Trying to Prognosticate the Future

Planning in an Uncertain Economy

Successfully Navigating Stormy Waters

Recession Resolutions

Bright Ideas

Innovative Marketing Ideas

Shape Up Your Selling Skills

Recession Hangovers

Hungry for Upbeat

Upbeat vs. Beat Up

"I'm not afraid of storms, for I'm learning to sail my ship."

Louisa May Alcott

THOSE LEMONS ARE GREAT FOR MAKING LEMONADE and lemon meringue pie...but, as I compile this book, we are in the third year of the most severe recession since the Great Depression. In fact, some parts of the country began to feel the dip 5 years ago. I've been through many dips—though none this precipitous—and I've seen what works and what doesn't in getting a remodeling company through successfully.

In general, I would encourage you to think that about every 5 years there will be a downturn of some sort in your part of the country. It may stem from the closing of a major business or even a major state industry, or it may be endemic to the entire country.

So surf (and make money) on the waves of prosperity and use your backup plans and your rainy day funds for when the sea is flat. Here are some hard-earned lessons from remodelers around the country that will stand you in good stead. They will help you shape your company during the next downturn.

The Mock Burial That Didn't Work

In September 1930, at the start of the Great Depression, businesspeople and politicians gathered in Cape Charles, Va., to perform a mock burial. Caskets containing "Old Man Business Depression," his wife, "Mrs. Pessimism," and his daughter, "Miss Misfortune," were unceremoniously dumped in a watery grave in the Chesapeake Bay. Unfortunately, while temporarily lifting the spirits of the onlookers, this act did nothing to end those troubled times.

Here we are in the Great Recession. We can do all the burying we want, but none of us—including our government—has an economic crystal ball. So how can we plan our future effectively?

I've got some ideas, but remember that all consultants have their biases. I tend to be conservative and value safety and security over big risks that lead to big wins or watery graves. My guts tell me that we'll have a very slow, somewhat rocky recovery and that in the 5-year time frame we won't see a rebound to anywhere near our previous levels. Maybe by 10 years out we will see a significant loosening of the consumer's purse and credit availability.

So I would plan very carefully, with multiple scenarios and would be predicting a year much like the previous with a 5 to 10% loosening of leads and sales. Because of the uncertainty, I would focus on *short-term planning* and make monitoring and updating those plans my best weapon in such uncertainty.

I've just come from a meeting of 30 of our clients, who tend to be top remodelers. They come from all over North America. While this isn't a scientific survey, it may help you in planning.

Of the clients at the meeting, 5 to 8% are doing well, have enough work, and have some backlog of unstarted work. A number of those are in Canada, where the recession has been milder. Most are working harder than ever with fewer leads, a poorer closing ratio (1 out of 8 vs. 1 out of 5), and smaller job sizes.

All of the remodelers now recognize that *marketing* must be a critical component of running their businesses. While it used to be a matter of pride to say "all my leads come from referrals," that referral base today cannot support the company. While marketing expenditures of 1 to 2% were common, it now takes 4 to 5% of your projected volume to deliver a marketing plan that will support your downsized company.

Marketing that works includes making clients deliriously happy with your work and substantiating that with third-party surveying—that's your base. It also includes marketing back to your referral base six times a year with a variety pack of communications, events, and programs. Climbing high on the marketing hit parade is belly-to-belly marketing, where you and your staff work in key organizations in your community.

You may even create your own networking group that agrees to exchange leads between top-quality companies. You want to have your "elevator" speech ready about your company and be out-front but not obnoxious about letting everyone (yes, *everyone*) know what you do. Meanwhile, you've got to be upgrading your website and optimizing how high it appears on search engines. Online newsletters still appear to be effective, but you need to have gathered e-mail addresses for your database.

Marketing outreaches that are much, much weaker now include newsletters, postcards, and virtually any mass mailing. I'm still not a fan of Yellow Pages, except for phone listings (although more and more folks are using their phones and online to get listings). Yellow Pages do work for trade contractors and specialty companies. Magazine ads usually do not work and newspaper ads are expensive and usually a bust. The jury is still out on pay-per-click search engines and that would normally be a tactic only for a multi-million dollar remodeler.

So get planning and involve your staff—the bigger the brain trust, the better. It should be an exciting ride.

Trying to Prognosticate the Future

How do you gauge what the coming year will be like economically? For some remodelers, it is staying in touch with bankers, accountants, real estate brokers, suppliers, subs, architects, and other remodelers. Or you may watch job growth or loss in your market area. Whatever you choose, you do need a way to monitor the economic health of your market.

For me, the first rumblings came from a group of 20 remodelers from around the country discussing their local economies. The upshot of the discussion was that there still were enough leads coming in, but their markets seemed softer than they had been. It was enough to make these remodelers question what was going on with their potential clients' buying decisions. A number noted that high-priced homes were selling only sluggishly and that inventory was mounting for those homes. Were the well-to-do getting uneasy?

A few weeks later at a local association meeting, there were a number of remodelers telling anecdotal stories of job sizes dropping, causing companies who'd previously had a minimum job-size requirement to drop that floor to smaller size jobs.

But what has really caught my attention was the latest quarterly survey by the McDonald Financial Group, which showed that the confidence wealthy consumers have in the economy fell to a 30-month low. The survey polls approximately 400 consumers who have annual incomes of over $150,000 or have more than $500,000 in investments, not including their home. For most remodelers, these consumers form the base of their prime buyers.

Fifty-seven percent of those surveyed said the economy is headed in the wrong direction and only 15% believed the economy would improve over the next 3 months.

What might this mean to you? Tie this in with reports that many of the hottest real estate markets around the country are cooling, and you've got signals that your business planning for next year should be on the conservative side. Consider doing three plans and budgets—one for what might be normal growth for your company, one for a 10 to 15% drop-off, and the last for a 25% drop-off in revenue.

Here are some tips I've learned from past slowdowns:

➤ Watch your intake process like a hawk. Try to establish comfortable dollar-volume benchmarks for projects in design, in estimating, and in sold-construction backlog. That will give you an early warning if there is a slowdown.

➤ Typically, remodelers don't react quickly enough to a slump. They don't have a backup plan and don't cut overhead and field staff until too late. That eats up your backlog and puts the entire company in danger.

➤ Your average job size will drop because your clientele will get more conservative about their spending. The smaller your average job size, the higher the overhead impact.

➤ Cash in the company pipeline will get tighter as your backlog (and deposits) get used up. You will need to have better reserves just when the economy makes it tougher to have them.

➤ It will be very tempting to cut marketing but while marketing will yield less than normal, it will be critical to keeping your name in front of your community. You will likely need to up your marketing dollars as a percentage of your volume.

Believe it or not, there are even a few plusses that result from a downturn if you are prepared to take advantage of them:

By being able to hold on, you will gain market share and be wonderfully positioned as the economy revives.

This is definitely a chance for you to get rid of inefficiency and fat in your company. You'll want to use this opportunity to "free up the future" of any marginal employees. You'll want to examine every line item in your overhead budget to see what can be negotiated down (rents, insurance, services?).

It will be easier than it has been in a long time to hire good folks to build your company's strengths.

It's all about preparing for the worst while hoping for the best.

Planning in an Uncertain Economy

It's always refreshing to turn over a new year. We get a fresh start and a clean slate. As each year unfolds, it gives us clues as to which direction the economy is going to take and how fast it will move.

If your business is starting this year right, you've already done your planning for the year. You have updated your business plan, have at least two budgets in place (reasonable but reaching budget and a less optimistic fallback budget), and have outlined your marketing for the year.

A good marketing plan includes a list of main goals or strategies, the tactics that will support those goals, a line-item budget, a calendar of activities, and a good monitoring system. Marketing has become very high priority in these times when our referral base simply can't support us by itself.

Here are some planning tips from the consulting trenches:

I'm recommending that my clients shorten their planning horizon until we can get some sense of where the economy is going. However, I have been asking what their 5-year vision is so that we can aim in that direction. We are not trying to fully flesh out 5- or 10-year plans at this point because the economy is too uncertain.

I'm also being very conservative about what—at best—we can expect in remodeling business volume and margins in the next year. In asking for at least two budgets, I'm suggesting that the reasonable but reaching budget figure a 5 to 10% improvement in remodeling volume and the fallback budget figure a volume similar to last year. Obviously there are reasons to raise or lower expectations, such as a good backlog of work signed and ready to start this year or a large job last year that you don't expect to be able to replicate this year. If you want to play with more optimistic projections you can do as many budgets as you want, but these two are musts.

When the remodeler I am working with tends to be optimistic and has a record of overestimating volume projections, I am definitely trying to bring them down to earth. When you overestimate your volume and miss, you typically have a losing year because your overhead is predicated on your volume.

I watch out for owners who sell, which includes most company owners. In my experience, they often paint too bright a picture to their company's detriment.

And speaking of overhead, I saw remodeler after remodeler have a losing or breakeven year last year because as volume didn't meet their projection, they refused to trim overhead. Most remodelers have now used up any cash cushion and really have to be sure the company lives within its means. That may well mean that staff has to be reduced or hours or salaries must be cut.

It's important to remember that budgets are tools. They aren't static. They aren't written in concrete. They need to be monitored monthly and changes made as needed but at least quarterly. If you see you've underestimated volume, overestimated gross profit, or are getting by with fewer staff, rework your budget up or down.

Use trigger points—unemotional metrics set within a time frame—that tell you that you need to move to your fallback (or worse) budget. For instance, you may decide that if you don't have 20% of your projected volume sold by the end of the first quarter that you will make three defined cuts, or that if the big Harris project doesn't sell by March 1, that you'll take certain actions. Pre-thinking these decision points will make them easier and less emotional when the time comes.

Folks, survival today is all about planning carefully, following the plan, and taking decisive action as needed. That old quote "Fail to plan and you plan to fail," has never been truer.

Successfully Navigating Stormy Waters

"We have shrunk back to $3,000,000 from $6,700,000 and have remained profitable every year and plan to do it again this year," writes one of my clients.

Congratulations to this company for successfully navigating very difficult waters. It has been clear in this recession that staying profitable while volume expands is far easier than staying profitable while it contracts.

Why is downsizing so difficult?

There are a number of reasons. As the company grows we invest in employees, many of whom are "keepers." We plan to build our future on those team members because we know they will scale up with the company's progress. As we must decrease overhead to scale back, it is so difficult to let these folks go. It is much easier to rationalize a faster uptick than actually emerges. When we build an overhead for an overly optimistic volume that never materializes, we are headed for a losing year. And most companies today do not have the self-financing to support losses over multiple years.

A second reason scaling down is hard to do is organizational. We have hired people to specialize in a $7,000,000 company and they often can't do the multi-tasking and play the multiple roles that a smaller company size demands. Thus, even if we cut our team numbers, we may not have the right players left to succeed in changed roles.

Downsizing has a double meaning with this recession—volume for most companies is less but job size is also smaller. That means more work to sell each bit of volume and if we don't streamline our processes for the new reality, we may be overwhelmed with work, appear to need all our team, and find ourselves at breakeven or worse.

Downsizing may also represent (at least temporarily) the death of a dream for the owner of the company. Having the larger volume may mean the owner no longer needs to play a day-to-day role in the company but can stay in the leadership/management role.

Or it may mean the owner is able to concentrate on sales and leave production to a production manager. Or the larger volume may be a big step toward the company's self-sufficiency that will free the owner to accomplish other goals that they have. The slap of the recession and the need to cut, cut, cut may be a tremendous blow to the owner and may necessitate steps they simply choose to ignore.

What does it take to downsize effectively and be profitable while doing it? Simply said, it takes a detailed plan and that plan is your budget(s). At all times, you and your key management team must know your anticipated volume (be as realistic here as you can), your expected job costs (by percentage, not by category), your overhead (highly detailed by line item), and your anticipated net profit (do whatever you have to do in the overhead category to allow for an 8% net after owner salary).

You may feel better if you do three budget scenarios, as we like to recommend to our clients. One is for a volume that is slightly better (+10%?) than you would realistically bet on at this time. The second is the realistic budget, and the third is the "fallback" or worst-case-scenario budget where your volume or your gross profit is 10% poorer than you currently anticipate. This third budget would include decision triggers at which point you would take certain actions to bring overhead into line with that budget.

Once you have developed the budgets you can believe in, separate the realistic one down to monthly income projections and expenditures. Don't simply divide each item by 12 but actually research how and when you expect your income and expenses to fluctuate. This can be entered into your accounting software and a monthly budget-to-actual report generated for your company. You would receive this report along with your P&L each month and it would alert you to key variances.

One area to be particularly aware of is budgeting your marketing. There has been a major change in the amount remodelers need to spend for adequate marketing. The budget used to be 1 to 2% and now is 4 to 5% for full-line remodelers.

Then, with plan(s) in hand, all you need to do is review those monthly P&Ls, do a budget reconciliation at least quarterly, and keep your company on track with your best friend in a recession—your budget.

Recession Resolutions

This recession has truly been cataclysmic for most remodelers. Learning just how bad the economic weather can get undoubtedly has taught all of us many enduring lessons. I set out to ask remodelers what they learned while surviving this recession that they want to be sure they remember when better times return. They all had ready answers and those answers were quite diverse.

Increased emphasis on marketing.
The majority chimed in on this topic—understandable because the recession totally upended what had been working in lead generation for remodelers.

For Mike McCutcheon, owner of McCutcheon Construction in Berkeley, Calif., hard times meant recognizing the power of the relationships that support a business in good times and bad. "All the electronic and print contact in the world is no substitute for simple face-to-face human contact," says McCutcheon. "Customers love it, employees love it, designers love it, and it is the only 'magic bullet' that is truly magic."

Rob Baugher of Baugher Design & Remodel Inc., in Homewood, Ala., formed tighter relationships by taking his vendors to lunch to "encourage them and see if there was something we could do together to increase the work flow." Many told him they had never been asked to lunch by a contractor. "We thought up new ideas—some worked and some didn't," Baugher said. "Our network began to contact us first when they heard about a project. We learned that we are stronger when we work as a team than when we work alone. We should have already known that."

Continuing to market even if the expenditure becomes a bigger percentage of overhead as volume drops is Andrew Shore's mantra for the future. The owner of Sea Pointe Construction in Irvine, Calif., counsels staying on top of what's working because "marketing involves continual learning." Baugher also doubled the quantity of his marketing to offset the reduced number of leads he anticipated.

Assuring financial stability.

Using longer term reports and watching for trends can give a remodeler an earlier warning of an oncoming problem. His monthly WIP (work in progress) report showed Baugher that "there was a problem coming." He's now looking at using longer term reports—a 12-month rolling average—to track vital financial details.

The critical financial lesson for Jay Cipriani of Cipriani Builders in Woodbury, N.J., is to "always have a plan B." While they used to plan for a physical disaster like an office fire, Cipriani says, "Now we need to think beyond the physical emergency to the economic meltdown." Shore wants not just two plans but three for two positive scenarios and one fallback, worst-case scenario. "That gives you a plan you can be continually monitoring and watching," he advises.

"Stay lean and keep a cash reserve because you never know what's coming," advises Shore. "I had a sense that a downturn was coming, so I had stockpiled some money and that has been key to our weathering the storm."

Wider diversification of services.

The recession has taught Shore that, "we needed to broaden our appeal from our upper middle-class market." Recognizing that those folks are in tight financial times, the remodeler moved to a higher income demographic. "We are sustained by those folks who still have money and are willing to spend it," says Shore.

While VB Homes in Newport News, Va., was already diversified with new home building and remodeling, partner Chancy Walker is emphatic that they still need more types of work to create a solid base for the company in all economic times. "For years, we have been turning down small jobs and referring them to others," he says. "Now we are making a strong effort to market ourselves as the company that can meet all our clients' and our marketplace's needs."

Vincent D'Avena of A.V. Remodeling and Construction in McLean, Va., quickly saw that he needed to reposition his firm for survival as well as long-term growth. "We've developed into a solid design firm and now sell more design remodel projects than competitive bids," says the remodeler. He is developing expertise in aging-in-place and green building.

Leaner staffing.

VB Homes' Walker expresses a common sentiment. "We had indulged ourselves and allowed overhead personnel to grow," he says. "Now we know we can do more with less as well as ask for more from our team members."

Cipriani has always used the "is it a need or a want?" with his client's wishes. Now he vows to apply it to staffing. He says, "We've learned we can do just as much with fewer people. It was convenient to have extra people do extra tasks, but that was not a good financial decision."

None of the remodelers I spoke with were depressed. They even seemed invigorated by playing a very tough game and seemed to recognize that the game was far from over. There was a confidence that they had adjusted to the new rules and would survive. D'Avena summed it up, "The bottom line is that we've listened more, focused on being nimble and flexible and positioning ourselves as best we can to catapult with the market as things turn around."

Bright Ideas

Here's the word from the remodelers we talk with from around the country—phones are ringing more and jobs are selling. There's still a lack of urgency from the buyer and job sizes are smaller with more practical scopes of work. A few—but very few—of our clients have all the work they need. Overall, things are looking up.

That doesn't mean every remodeler is in great shape. Here's a checklist of ideas that have helped our clients keep their businesses healthy and on track during this economic storm.

Are you...
Keeping spirits high, including your own?
This is a tough but critical factor. Your staff has to see light at the end of the tunnel to work hard. It's up to you as owner to carry the banner, keep everyone focused on the vision, and communicate that their work is significant. Owners need first to keep themselves in shape with reasonable working hours, good exercise, and occasional getaways.

At the office, celebrate even small wins. Use sincere praise lavishly. Turn goals into games that can be won with small non-monetary prizes (for example, a family barbeque party served by you).

Using today's marketing?
That means an enhanced budget that is likely to be 4 to 5% of your projected company volume rather than yesterday's 1%. Marketing has moved from a sometime thing to priority status. It means spending that money wisely with a good diversified mix that emphasizes person-to-person contact like seminars, home tours, and active membership in the organizations that attract your prospective clients. With that increased expenditure and the ability to hone the marketing you are doing, keeping great statistics has become key. You should know how much each lead, appointment, and job from a particular source costs you.

Make sure your website is optimized for searching by prospects (check it out for free on www.websitegrader.com). Be sure your website is showing not just the budget-buster, award-winning jobs you do but also the moderate-budget projects that prospects may be contemplating.

And be sure your database of past clients and friends of the company are hearing from you regularly. After all, they buy again and most importantly, they are your true sales force—but only if you stay top-of-mind with them.

Returning to highly professional consultative selling?
Yesterday's slap-dash order taking just doesn't work anymore. And the recession panic that led you to reduced qualifying that led you to visiting every lead and throwing an estimate at them is your worst enemy. Today's tough sales climate means going back to the basics. Rethink your sales process with the information you have learned in the last 2 years. Renew yourself by getting training in person or via the web, books, or CDs.

It may sound strange, but qualifying is more important than ever to keep you from feeling like that proverbial guinea pig on the never-ending exercise wheel. If you're a worn-out salesperson, you are a goner.

Go back to qualifying, to weeding out at the first appointment so that you don't promise an "estimate" to someone you know won't buy or who doesn't have reasonably precise specs. Save your best for those who fit the profile of your buyer and give them your very best service. If they don't buy immediately, find ways to stay in touch.

Scouring overhead for every penny in savings?
Get your entire team on this one. Review every line in your budget. There may be some items that can be dispensed with entirely. On others, I'm hearing our clients successfully renegotiating rent, insurance costs, photography costs, and accounting fees. Nothing is sacred. It doesn't hurt to ask.

Do you have extra building space that could be rented? Or should you be moving back to a home office or a shared office?

Building the "A" team?
Hopefully you've gotten rid of any "C" players on your team and if anyone else needs to go, focus on the "B" players. If you've been killing yourself to try

to save your staff and you've used up any savings you have, it is time to seriously reevaluate that policy. Would it be better to reduce salaries overall, including yours? Or would it be preferable to let someone go? On the other hand, if you need to fill a position, there are great people looking for work. This is the time to hire, but only if you actually need them today. I'm hearing good things about ads on Craig's List.

Tightening up every bit of leakage in estimating and production?

If you haven't renegotiated with your vendors and trade contractors, now is the time to do it. You may want to find some additional trade contractors while their workload is down. Talk to your major vendors and see if they will add a few percentage points to your discount, give you a quick-pay discount, or negotiate for co-op money for your marketing.

Have you considered subcontracting all or part of your carpentry? We used to think it couldn't be done and still keep quality high, but more and more top quality remodelers are proving that thinking is just plain wrong. By subcontracting more, a greater percentage of your estimate costs are fixed and you are able to better adjust as work ebbs and flows.

As your job sizes drop, the complexity of your systems need to simplify. Are you reviewing how to fast-track projects, especially those of handyman size? If not you may be spending too much precious overhead on too little potential gross profit.

Innovative Marketing Ideas

Reports from our clients and remodeler friends continue to fly into our office about major cuts in personnel and how devastatingly hard the decision and implementation is.

But the mourning is short as each company learns to cope. There is an exhilaration in doing more with less. That old remodeling "can do" attitude merges with "we *will* do" to create new solutions and new outreaches. The personnel who remain are more engaged and committed, willing to take on multiple hats and new tasks.

Much of the new thinking is about how to approach marketing for quality leads. It seems that spending money is much less fruitful, even if you have that money available. Those postcards, paper newsletters, ads in magazines, and newspapers just aren't paying their way.

Spending time is where the payoff is today. We call it belly-to-belly marketing. You and your staff have to go out and meet and greet. Every contact you make and every conversation you have has the possibility of a job lurking nearby. All of us have to be subtle gold miners looking for the next small vein of work.

Here are some of the unusual marketing outreaches savvy remodelers are devising. For each, there is a useful takeaway lesson that might help you with your marketing outreach.

Targeting advertising to big-game hunters.

"We will have a program ad and will sponsor a day's carpentry services for the next Safari Club International local chapter fund-raising banquet," says Jerry Liu of D.G. Liu Contractor, Inc., in Dickerson, Md. "Our ad will feature photos of trophy rooms we have built. I am hoping that any prospect that is still traveling overseas to hunt is still spending and may spend with us. Instead of avoiding the subject for fear of offending someone, our outdoor passion becomes a bonding and rapport tool."

> *Takeaway:* Maximize your unique opportunities to get in front of those who have discretionary spending potential.

Holding a seminar at a home furnishings store.

Jeff and Adele Talmadge of Talmadge Construction, Inc., in Aptos, Calif., have been doing seminars for the public and now have a special opportunity. They are co-oping the next one with a financial advisor at a nearby high-end home furnishings store. The topic is "There is No Place Like Home: Remodeling for a Vibrant Aging Population," and, because three companies are involved, costs will be greatly reduced.

> *Takeaway:* Brainstorm how to co-op with other businesses that would like to have more belly-to-belly contact with prospects in an educational setting. Share client lists. What businesses would like to gather a group of people in their showroom to potentially impulse-buy?

Hosting an Open House.

"We recently completed a whole-house remodel and are co-hosting an open house with the homeowners for all the folks who worked on their home," says Amy O'Brien, marketing director at Agape Construction Company in Kirkwood, Mo. "They are also going to let us invite some prospects to this open house. We have found this to be one of the best ways to get people we are working with to pull the trigger and sign the contract."

> *Takeaway:* Bringing folks who are thinking about working with you into a beautiful, completed project to meet your staff and your happy clients creates a natural and powerful selling situation.

Circling the wagons.

Think pioneers and Indians here. Amie Riggs, CGR, CAPS, of Riggs Construction Company Inc., in Kirkwood, Mo., says, "Our company has started a group called The Riggs Remodeling Leadership Group. Members are our preferred contractors and suppliers. The focus is to create leads for each other. After the first meeting, I received three viable leads from two different members. If we have work, so will the other members."

> *Takeaway:* The remodeling pie is smaller. Let's save all the pieces for folks in our network who can cross refer work to us. We want our best trade contractors and suppliers to survive.

Hold your own networking event.

"We hosted an event called Ben's Better Business After Hours at our office," reports Ben Thompson, CGR, GCP, of Thompson Remodeling, Inc., in Grand Rapids, Mich. "Over 42 people came! Parking was a nightmare...it was awesome! Business will be written from connections made by my guests. This can only help TRI.

"I spent $400 on catering excellent food and $100 on locally roasted coffee and caramel apple cider latte service. The door prize was a free carpenter for a day (totally transferable to whomever they choose to give the service to, or lunch at the restaurant of their choosing). Everyone there had my stamp of approval/endorsement, and I hope that is what paved the way for the wonderful conversations, introductions, and passed referrals we all participated in. Multiple past clients came too!"

> *Takeaway:* I'll let Ben Thompson say it in his own words. "I've been asking myself what I can do to add value to the world I work in that no one else can do. Here's what I know I can do. I can connect the people I am connected with."

Today, you've got to be willing to break out of the marketing box. If it works, keep it. If it doesn't, move on. And remember—belly-to-belly!

Shape Up Your Selling Skills

This less-than-healthy remodeling market has spawned a number of tough sales challenges. There are fewer leads and weaker leads, and there is more competitive pressure from home builders and warier prospects.

Yet I've watched many remodelers under the pressure of this market actually reduce the effectiveness of their selling by making the following mistakes:

➤ Performing minimal or no qualification in hopes that somewhere in the stack of weak leads may lay a job.

➤ Franticly making appointments day and night.

➤ E-mailing proposals in lieu of second visits because they are working so many leads.

➤ Log-jamming their design/estimating systems because they are going for quantity, not quality.

➤ Decreasing design-to-construction conversions—partly a result of the market but largely by ever-longer design cycles, by reducing design fees (thus, in some cases, attracting less-dedicated buyers), and by not carefully servicing those prospects in the system.

We will now look back on the past years as golden years for remodeling, as a time when remodelers could succeed as "order takers." Tough times like these mean a return to true selling, to going back to the basics.

So what's working in sales?

Slow hiring.

Smart remodelers are getting very serious about not only who they hire to sell for the company but how they hire them. They are developing hiring packages that include search criteria (what skills, abilities, talents, and experience do we want this person to have?), job descriptions, interview questions, and compensation packages that mirror the company's culture. The good news is that the job market is weak and I am hearing reports of amazing hires—especially from online ads. If you need a key player, this is the time to get them.

Sales boot camp.

Savvy remodelers are developing sales training systems for the first 30, 60, and 90 days for the new sales hire. In some cases this includes outside training, but often it is home grown. It includes learning about the company and its systems, shadowing established salespeople, role playing, weekly meetings, and reading books or listening to CDs.

Fast firing.

Remodelers are deciding—ahead of time—what the pass/fail criteria are for a new hire to stay past 30, 60, and 90 days. What behaviors will be measured and monitored for fit with the company system? How many first appointments, presentations, and sales are required per month?

Team selling.

I'm hearing more and more favorable reviews about team selling, especially when the sales team includes a man and a woman. The team might pair a salesperson and a designer and one will be responsible for keeping very tight and accurate notes. Often, the salesperson is the owner of the company and by having a second person at the initial meetings, the handoff to a design team is very smooth. This team selling is definitely a differentiator between you and your competition.

Selling fast.

A number of remodelers are successful with getting design agreements signed on the first visit—not always by any means, but sometimes. Otherwise, they leave the design agreement and follow up. This requires the ability to give good budget ballpark ranges for the proposed scope.

Prospect coddling.

Strangely, while we need jobs more than ever, many remodelers are losing momentum and prospect satisfaction with how they are handling prospective jobs between the design agreement paperwork and the sale, thus lowering urgency and conversion to the construction contract. In some cases, this comes from reducing staff, or a lack of urgency on the part of the prospect, or not controlling the design process. Why not hold a meeting of your sales/design/estimating staff focusing on your process from the prospect's point of view and how to streamline it? Then take the best ideas and put them into place.

Rehashing as an art form.

Remodelers are pulling out their old lead sheets and calling to assess whether folks have done the job or are still holding. The hope with doing this is to revive some of these leads. It's also a good time to find out how they were handled by your company the first time around. And for that reason, I would have someone call who is very good on the phone and is not the original salesperson. You definitely want to do this with lost design clients as well.

So the news is mixed. What we do know is that it is time to go back to the solid sales basics and rebuild your sales system if it has gotten off track. You will look back at this recession as a time of relearning, of getting lean and doing more with less. And you'll be ready to take on the world as the market revs up.

Recession Hangovers

As I listen to the drumbeat of economic news and predictions, I'm beginning to hear a refrain—that if we think (and plan) as though our buyers are going to return to unrestrained spending when this recession is over, we may be planning on quicksand.

For any of us who knew folks who had lived thru the 1930's depression, their frugality was legendary. They saved those tiny bits of soap remnants, reused envelopes for making lists, and put aside money religiously for a rainy day. Even though the Great Depression may have been 40 or 50 years back for them, they never forgot the lesson of how bad it could get and how fast it could get bad. Nor will we.

The hypothesis that is being written and spoken about is that, while this recession is unlikely to be as bad as the Great Depression, it will have a lasting effect on buying habits even as joblessness improves, credit frees up, and home prices improve. Entire generations may rethink and change their buying patterns.

An article called "Understanding the Post-Recession Consumer" in the *Harvard Business Review* (July-August 2009) by Paul Flatters and Michael Wilmott puts some meat and detail on that hypothesis. The authors are trend trackers and the article lays out the trends they feel are accelerating and those they feel are slowing. A number are food for thought for remodelers.

Among their accelerating trends is *discretionary thrift*. While some consumers must be thrifty because of their lower incomes, this habit is now extending to many affluent buyers who "desire a more wholesome and less wasteful life," note the authors. They go on to write that, "Many post-recession purchases, we suspect, will be less extravagant versions of the originals." If this trend takes place, it would appear that our remodeling consumers will want fewer frills, maybe even less extravagant square footage and more value for their dollar.

Along with discretionary thrift, the authors predict a dominant and lasting trend will be a *demand for simplicity*, which will help to reduce stress. This may bode well for those remodelers who can simplify the buying process, streamline the delivery, and package their services very clearly.

A trend the authors see as at least temporarily slowing is *green consumerism* due to the often more expensive price tag on green products. However, Flatters and Wilmott, "expect green consumerism to recover and accelerate post-recession …as consumers regain confidence and disposable income to fully express their growing concern about climate change and the environment." Many remodelers are selling sustainability because they are passionate about good environmentalism. Others are beginning to tout green because they believe it is fashionable or will help them sell. A temporary dip may well move them out of the market.

A second article, "Selling to the Debt-Averse Consumer," by Eric Janszen in the same issue of the *Harvard Business Review* suggests that companies will have to figure out "how to make do without the former life of the economic party: the monthly payer."

While not all remodelers involve themselves in the financing side of the business, many of their jobs are made possible by financing that the consumer obtains. Janszen advises—much like the previous authors—that, "Messages that center on family, life simplification, and getting back to basics will appeal."

The point is that the effects of this recession will be with us for the next decade, if not longer. It's clear that no one knows when our economy will be back on the road to health and what the long-term fallout will be from generations of people learning that the stock market does not always go up, that even if they do a good job they may not keep their job, that houses do not always rise in value, and that much of what they buy they do not need.

And that means we all have to become sleuths to stay up on just what messages those jungle drums are sending. Here are some ideas:

1. Gather economic information everywhere and all the time. In a month's time, you can chat with a hundred sources in your market—your banker, your accountant, your plumber, your grocer, and your fellow remodelers. Make a habit of finding out how things are going in your market.

2. Find some publications (paper or online) like *Remodeling* magazine as well as those that address general business (I like *Inc.* magazine and *Harvard Business Review*) that you trust and take time to read them. In today's fast-changing market, books may be too slow for gathering up-to-date economic information.

3. As you make changes in your company structure, offerings, and systems, focus on simplification, and being user-friendly, efficient, economic, and value-focused. Make changes that will work for you and your buyers in the long run.

Hungry for Upbeat

Capers Café in the Portland, Ore., airport made me realize just how hungry I was—and not for food. I was there for an early breakfast before my cross-country flight. Going through the order line, I was complimented twice by staff.

There I was in an airport, ready to fly—ready for rudeness, impersonality, too little space, and no privacy. And all of a sudden, things were looking up. And what did it take? A couple of compliments and a few smiling faces. For a few moments, Capers Café was able to break through and make me smile and enjoy what I didn't expect to enjoy. I was hungry for upbeat. And I got it as a bonus with my breakfast. I will look forward to anytime that I can return.

We're all beat up right now. We have less money than we thought we had. We stop and think before every purchase. It's just more complicated. A large purchase—like remodeling—means examining our conscience for whether we can afford to spend the money, whether we should spend the money, what will the impact be on the value of our home, whether our neighbors will talk disparagingly about our expenditure, and whether what we do will be good for the earth. And over and above that, we've been taught (or learned) that remodeling is hell.

I wish I had the magic answer to make your prospects turn into clients and your clients turn into loyalists. I don't. But I can tell you that friendliness, courtesy, and good humor will definitely help and that they can be institutionalized in your company.

It certainly won't hurt your staff, either. Your staff is worried—about losing their jobs and about losing their homes plus all the usual worries of sick children, elderly parents, and more. Having a job where good humor and care for each another reigns is quite a tonic and will make your company a magnet for new hires.

Let's go back to Capers Café. That was my second visit there. The English lady taking my order remarked on my purple sweater set. My mood immediately rose a couple of points. Then I remembered this lady from my previous trip. Why? Because she complimented me then.

The next compliment—on my jazzy glasses—came as I paid for my meal. Again, I remembered that it was exactly the same white-haired lady who accepted my money before—and who complimented me on my previous visit to the café. But still, these seemed to be compliments delivered sincerely about objects I really liked. I decided to become a detective and learn more.

As I discreetly fixed my coffee just a few steps away from the cashier, I heard her deliver one mood-boosting comment to each patron. Her comments seemed to be sincere, but I assumed she was always searching for a legitimate reason to compliment. Nothing was forced. Nothing seemed fake. I thought back to reading *The One Minute Manager* by Ken Blanchard and his phrase "Catch people doing something right."

I had plenty of time before my flight, and I was curious. What was going on there? As I ate my breakfast, I watched the wait staff deliver a friendly, upbeat, and customized, client-focused ballet in such an impersonal and unexpected setting.

I pulled over a busboy and learned his name was Matthew. "What special qualities do you have to have to be hired here?" I asked.

"None really," Matthew replied, "but you do have to have an ability to work with stressed customers. This is a great place to work. You can't be up everyday, but if I'm not, my co-workers will inspire me."

"Is it that you've come into a culture that encourages a certain kind of positive behavior?" I asked.

"Definitely," Matthew said, and moved on.

It's probably past time for you to do a good culture check on your company. How would your folks rate your mood (or moodiness?) You are the model that everyone will follow. What's going on in the fun department for staff and clients alike? How energetically is your phone answered? If you have an office or showroom open to the public, watch how folks are greeted—maybe they are offered coffee or a soda. Brainstorm on how you can take where you are today on the "good news" scale and move it up a notch or two.

You've probably seen that television commercial that shows one good deed after another inspired by the one before. Be the inspirer, the beacon—and I don't know when or where—but it will bring you clients who will turn into loyalists.

Upbeat vs. Beat Up

Everywhere I go, no matter who I speak with, there is fallout from the economy: unemployed friends and relatives, sinking businesses, reduced consumption, and so much more. Just how have some business owners managed to stay upbeat yet focused? How do they lead with vigor in a way that inspires their staff to follow them with confidence?

Pumped by the Mission

I started these conversations by talking with my partner, Victoria Downing, president of Remodelers Advantage. When she walks in the office door each morning, she is met with calls and e-mails from remodelers who are in business trouble—and, occasionally, in personal trouble. Our business, like everyone else's, is down.

Yet, "I'm pumped by our mission—our ability to help our clients," Downing says. "The hunt for new sales keeps me upbeat, and there are many unexpected opportunities to try new things, to do more with less."

She also revels in casual dress, bringing her dog to the office, and being open to the possibility of unexpected fun. For instance, on one particularly difficult day before Christmas, the postman delivered a gift of two bottles of wine to the office. The staff gathered around, and one bottle was gone with lightning speed by 2 p.m. So, partying may be part of the mix as well.

Steve Jordan is president of Rebuilding America, in Pensacola, Fla., which partners with investors to rehab houses for rent. He's watching house values drop, rental prices drop, and vacancies rise. But he doesn't miss a beat and sees opportunities everywhere.

Every day, he makes a written list of the 10 things he is most grateful for. Having been in a 12-step program for 33 years, Jordan has this realistic attitude: "We each have 24 hours a day, and we can deal with anything if we deal with it for just one day at a time. When I try to forecast the future, I can talk myself into a depression." Instead, Jordan keeps to a schedule that includes meditation, a daily routine, and a strong work ethic, all of which stand him in especially good stead during difficult times.

Cut Budgets, Not Fun

As part of her formula for staying positive, Liz Wilder surrounds herself with appropriately upbeat books, music, and audio books. "I have to make sure I'm positive every day because there's a clear connection between my mood and the mood of everyone with whom I work," says the president of Anthony Wilder Design/Build, in Bethesda, Md.

She also swears by starting each day right, with meditation and time to play with her beloved dogs. "They bring things down to a happy reality," she says.

Wilder also makes certain that the workday for her staff is full of fun and that good news of all types travels quickly—news of awards, signed contracts, inspirational quotes, and more. She notes that the latest all-company meeting took place at the office and was "catered" by Dunkin Donuts rather than being held as it once was at the nearby country club. There's a lesson—cut budgets, but never cut fun and celebration.

For each of us, there is a key to staying balanced. As another remodeler recently wrote to me, "My wife and I are looking forward to our kids and our one grandchild visiting soon. When I hear 'Grandpa!' called out at the baggage claim, all work worries will vaporize. The economy will do whatever it is going to do, the business may make or lose money, but the bottom line on my family investment is always positive."

My pep-ups are my two Jack Russell terriers. Who can maintain morose with these leaping, unpredictable, have-fun-with-a-string dogs? I tend to eat when I'm down but stay true to twice-a-week training sessions at the gym, which take my mind to a totally different place—I think it's called pain. And best of all, when you live on a farm, nature constantly invites you to come and partake. A walk will always mean unexpected findings and sightings and a fresh perspective.

So what will do it for you? By keeping yourself strong and positive, you will have laid the most important groundwork for a strong and positive company.

Remodelers Advantage Roundtables
PEER GROUPS

You don't have to go it alone! **Remodelers Advantage Roundtables** is the industry's largest and fastest-growing peer group organization exclusively for remodelers.

Want to see how other successful Remodeling company owners run their businesses? Wish you could have someone who REALLY understands remodeling work on your company's issues with you?

Roundtables brings remodelers together in non-competitive "think tank" groups that collaborate on finding the absolute best solutions to help each other's businesses grow. Within each group, company-owners like you, guided by our top industry experts, share expertise freely to help their fellow remodelers save time, money, and reduce the stress we all know is part of the remodeling industry.

Our expert Facilitators have 75+ combined years experience in the Remodeling Industry

500 articles, white papers and more focused on the challenges Remodelers face.

7 industry best sellers including *Mastering the Business of Remodeling* and *The Remodelers Guide to Making and Managing Money*

1,000 examples of sales, marketing, production, and business management strategies which are working successfully today

100's of tactics used by Remodelers Advantage members to deliver profitability that is more than double most non-members

Dozens of seminars and educational programs presented at all major industry trade shows including The Remodeling Show, Journal of Light Construction, and more.

100's of coaching clients

1000+ members of the Remodelers Advantage Learning Community

100's of reviews of critical performance metrics including financials, marketing stats, and production details.

Enjoy greater rewards from all your hard work ... sooner! Become a member of our Remodelers Advantage Roundtables peer-group network and get the **support, insights, and tried-and-true ideas to achieve your personal and business goals faster than you ever thought possible.**

Ready to join? Visit *www.RoundtablesPeerGroups.com* to start today!

> "It is no secret that many of the best and strongest companies in the country are members of Remodelers Advantage." *J.K.*

What's behind our #1 rating?

Builders and remodelers across America rate our products #1 and know certain things to be true of CertainTeed.

For starters, we've been in the roofing business for over 100 years. **CertainTeed** offers you the broadest range of color and style choices. But it's not style over substance. You get roofing products made from the highest quality materials and backed by the strongest warranty program. It's our promise to you: quality made certain, satisfaction guaranteed.

The Top 5 reasons why roofing contractors are confident in **CertainTeed** products:

1. **Proven Protection™:** CertainTeed's fiberglass shingles have over twenty five years of proven results based on actual field experience.

2. **Superior Design:** Our products are heavier by design than our major competitors. We believe that additional shingle weight translates to greater durability.

3. **Third-Party Verification** (Unique to CertainTeed): Underwriters Laboratory independently verifies that ALL of our shingle products meet the quality standard of ASTM D3462 and the ASTM D7158 Class H wind test.

4. **Top Rated:** A leading consumer magazine rated Landmark as a **"BEST BUY"** for the second consecutive time. And CertainTeed products are consistently ranked #1 in building industry surveys.

5. **Complete Coverage:** CertainTeed's warranty protects against **ANY** manufacturing defects, including aesthetic defects. Most manufacturers do not cover aesthetics, but only cover defects that "adversely affect performance" or cause a leak.

The Contractor's EDGE™... programs that mean business:

CertainTeed Roofing offers the industry's best trade knowledge manuals and most meaningful credential programs.

Go to **www.certainteed.com/edge** to discover the business resources and rewards available to roofing contractors.

Choose CertainTeed products for all of your remodeling needs

You can be certain of the high-quality that blends performance and style – both you and your customers will appreciate the difference. To learn more about CertainTeed, please visit **www.certainteed.com or call 800-233-8990.**

remodeling

hanley▲wood

Thank you, Linda ...

... for being part of the REMODELING family for so many years. Your expertise and innovation helped to shape the industry.

We will all miss you.

From the staff of REMODELING magazine